BLACKBIRD

By the same author

Marked for Death: The First War in the Air

BLACKBIRD

A HISTORY OF THE
UNTOUCHABLE SPY PLANE

JAMES HAMILTON-PATERSON

PEGASUS BOOKS
NEW YORK LONDON

BLACKBIRD

Pegasus Books Ltd
148 West 37th Street, 13th Floor
New York, NY 10018

Copyright © 2017 by James Hamilton-Paterson

First Pegasus Books hardcover edition September 2017

ISBN: 978-1-68177-505-0

10 9 8 7 6 5 4 3 2 1

Printed in the United States of America
Distributed by W. W. Norton & Company, Inc.

CONTENTS

Dedication

This book is dedicated to John
Farley, OBE, AFC: consummate
engineer, teacher, writer and
gentleman, as well as one of
the world's great test pilots.

1. PARANOIA

MOST ACCOUNTS OF the SR-71 family of aircraft are designed for the specialist aero-buff or 'Haynes Manual' end of the market. The more popular tend to concentrate on the *wow!* factor of astonishing performance and often overlook that, like any other aircraft, the 'Blackbirds' were expressly designed to perform a specific function. This was to carry an assortment of cameras and sensors over a target at high altitude and speed, collect a mass of information and return safely with it for evaluation. The ability to break speed and other records was merely a by-product of the design and never remotely a goal in itself. Once the top-secret aircraft had been officially 'revealed' (in the jargon of the day), this capacity for shattering world records was adroitly used for popular support in bolstering the case for its continued survival in the face of Pentagon moves to terminate the project.

Also generally missing from such accounts is an other-than-cursory attempt to place the Blackbird in the wider context of Cold War geopolitics as well as of 1950s aerodynamic design. This was the period of the adolescent Jet Age, whose increasing speeds entailed a rapid and highly competitive expansion of aerodynamic knowledge. Aero industries on both sides of the Atlantic spawned great numbers of advanced, inventive and occasionally plain silly aircraft designs, all in the hopes of going ever faster and higher. It was a time of obsessive competition between countries and companies, of wastefully duplicated effort and amazing progress. It was also the period of burgeoning nuclear technology and rocketry conducted under conditions of near-hysterical secrecy.

A series of political crises fed into and nourished the mutually sustained paranoia that raged in NATO countries and the Soviet Bloc alike, to be seen at its most obsessive in the United States and the USSR. Among these crises were the downing of Francis Gary Powers in his U-2 spy plane over the USSR on 1 May 1960; the building of the Berlin Wall (1961); the CIA-sponsored fiasco of the Cuban Bay of Pigs invasion (1961); and the Cuban

Missile Crisis of late 1962. By 1964 paranoia had intensified to the point where only satire could adequately deal with it – most notably Stanley Kubrick's brilliant film of that year, *Dr. Strangelove.*

'I can no longer sit back and allow Communist infiltration to sap and impurify all of our precious bodily fluids,' Sterling Hayden remarks in his role as General Jack D. Ripper, commanding officer of an American Strategic Air Command (SAC) bomber base, who has decided off his own bat that his B-52s should carry out a pre-emptive strike against the Soviet Union. Paranoia reached out even to the Shepperton Studios in Surrey where the film was made. When some US Air Force officers were invited to view the set they reportedly went white as they inspected the mock-up of the B-52 cockpit, stunned by its accuracy. Kubrick was obliged to elicit the set designer's promise that no military secrets had been divulged, that his invention was based entirely on imagination and a photo on the cover of an SAC propaganda book (Mel Hunter's *Strategic Air Command*) that showed enough of a cockpit for him to be able to make plausible guesses at the rest of it, including the switchgear for the bomb-arming and recall procedures. 'Otherwise,' Kubrick told

A B-52 releasing a 'bomb train' over Vietnam, March 31 1967, during Operation Rolling Thunder. This now-venerable bomber served SAC from 1955 and will probably still be active in 20 years' time.

Ken Adam, the production designer, 'you and I may shortly be dragged off and investigated by the FBI.'

In its post-1945 emergence as a superpower, the United States felt its dominant position threatened solely by the USSR and by the ethos of 'godless Communism' it was convinced Russia was disseminating with stealth and guile throughout the less developed nations, especially in South East Asia, China and Latin America. When in November 1956 Nikita Khrushchev addressed some Western ambassadors in Moscow immediately after he had crushed the Hungarian Uprising he promised them, 'We will bury you!' This was both melodramatic and chilling and the United States had no doubt that it was in a nuclear arms race with the Soviets. Each side strove to progress from atom bombs to hydrogen bombs, from propeller-driven to jet bombers, from surface-to-air missiles (SAMs) to intercontinental ballistic missiles (ICBMs), up through the stratosphere and out into space. Intense secrecy shrouded anything to do with the military, especially any form of experimental aircraft, and above all with nuclear weapons and their delivery systems.

Behind all this lay the constant, nagging fear that all unbeknownst the other side could be stealing a march, might have bigger and better weapons even now being readied under wraps in remote testing grounds. This fear was sedulously fostered by careful propaganda and misinformation that found its way into press and broadcast reports. The crises referred to above were essentially political; but just as bad, if not worse, were those brought on by technological advances. To the arms race was added the space race when in October 1957 the USSR launched the world's first satellite, Sputnik. This shocked the United States and caused widespread panic throughout the US military and intelligence agencies as they agonised over the Soviets' apparent technical superiority. Thereafter the lead in various fields fluctuated from one side to the other. Take a single month in 1961:

12 April: Major Yuri Gagarin became the first man in space, orbiting Earth for 108 minutes in the five-ton Vostok. At a press conference later that day President Kennedy lamented seeing the US once again come second to the USSR in the space field, admitting ruefully 'it will be some time before we catch up'.

21 April: The United States captured the world record speed for controlled flight with the 3,074 mph (4,947 kph) achieved by an X-15 rocket-powered aircraft drop-launched from a B-52 bomber in a joint project of NASA, the Air Force and the Navy.

28 April: The USSR set a new world altitude record for an aircraft taking off and landing conventionally with a height of 113,891 feet (34,714 metres) achieved by G. Mussolov in a Ye-66A. His aircraft was a much-tweaked MiG-21 fighter using a rocket booster to take it beyond the point where its jet engine failed for lack of atmosphere to bite on. This was exactly the same principle that would be used by Chuck Yeager's equally modified Starfighter, the NF-104A with rocket booster that reached no higher than 108,700 feet on 10 December 1963 in an attempt that very nearly cost him his life.

In short, the atmosphere was grimly competitive as well as grimly secretive. Certainly in the United States much of the anxiety centred around two subjects that journalists, with the help of the military, soon turned into ongoing crises: 'the bomber gap' and 'the missile gap'. Thanks to newspapers and periodicals like *Time* magazine these took on dread significance. Did the Soviets really have a thousand new bombers that could outnumber as well as outfly their American counterparts? Might they also be racing to produce advanced ballistic missiles commensurate with their apparent superiority in rocketry? From every point of view – and especially from that of the Pentagon, the CIA and the White House – it became vital to know. Traditional ground-based agents and spies had their uses, but the Iron Curtain was drawn very tightly shut and the only clinching information would be that of aerial reconnaissance using cameras that could produce high-resolution images of things the Soviets couldn't easily hide such as factories, missile launchers, airfields, radar sites and even the Moscow May Day parades.

But there was a complicating behind-the-scenes factor to the United States' military posture (as there doubtless was in the USSR as well): the often bitter wrangling for budgetary advantage between the three services, not to mention between the companies competing for contracts to supply high-value military hardware such as aircraft. Above all there was the US military's occasionally fraught relationship with the CIA and other intelligence agencies, not to mention smouldering disagreements between the White House, the Department of Defense and various administration officials.

Particularly germane to our story of an American aircraft is the primary importance in the 1950s and 1960s of the United States Air Force and especially of its bomber wing, SAC (pronounced 'sack'). In the days before ICBMs went into service the delivery of America's nuclear threat depended on SAC's immense fleets of B-47s and B-52s. In 1961 a system code-named CHROME

A Boeing RB-47E Stratojet over Kansas. This was the reconnaissance version of the B-47 bomber that first flew in 1947 and whose swept wings and podded engines became the template for most future airliners.

DOME came into operation. Under this scheme twelve of SAC's B-52s fully laden with nuclear bombs were kept on constant airborne alert, flying towards a 'fail-safe' point just outside the Soviet border. When they reached it they would automatically turn back unless they received a coded Go signal that meant they were to proceed and bomb their predetermined Russian targets, the exact co-ordinates of which were locked in a safe aboard each aircraft.

The existence and even the very name of CHROME DOME (which remained operative until 1968) were highly classified, making it all the more astonishing that *Dr. Strangelove* replicated exactly this supposedly top-secret strategy. The film's brilliant writer, Terry Southern, must have been not just imaginative but remarkably well-informed. His cigar-chomping General Ripper was clearly based on the abrasive figure of Curtis LeMay, the general who commanded SAC throughout the 1950s and then went to the Pentagon as the Air Force Chief of Staff in 1961. LeMay's meteoric career in the Second World War had left him with a reputation for competence but also for dogged belligerence towards all who opposed him, particularly civilians up to and including the President. He was especially impatient with any idea of negotiating with the Russians ('the pantywaist option' to use his phrase), and at moments of crisis he favoured launching a pre-emptive nuclear strike against the USSR to settle their hash once and for all. 'If I see that the Russians are amassing their planes for an attack,' he was recorded as saying to Robert C. Sprague of the Office of Defense Mobilization in 1957, 'I'm going to knock the [expletive] out of them before they take off the ground.' 'But General LeMay,' Sprague replied, 'that's not national policy.' 'I don't care,' LeMay said. 'It's *my* policy. That's what I'm going to do.'[1] It was greatly to John F. Kennedy's credit that five years later he was able to face down LeMay during the Cuban Missile Crisis when his rogue general was insisting on SAC launching a strike on Soviet nuclear missile sites in Cuba: a strike we now know would have triggered a full-scale nuclear exchange. It was only by pulling rank and reminding LeMay that the President of the United States was also Commander-in-Chief of the Armed Forces that Kennedy was able to prevail. By some accounts it was a close-run thing.

The importance of this bullish element in the
Air Force's high command will become apparent,
together with its often uneasy rivalry with civilian
intelligence-gathering agencies such as the CIA
over who should command and fly the fleet of
American spy planes. Indeed, it was the USAF high
command that finally ensured the Blackbirds were
axed with years of airframe life still left in them.
Similarly, the Pentagon's and the Air Force's impa-
tience with President Eisenhower and then with
President Kennedy over their frequent suspension
of all U-2 spy flights over the USSR in favour of
diplomacy led to deep frustration on the part of
the military. One can see their point, in that they
were in the dark about the exact capabilities of
the enemy they faced. They needed hard information about the Russians' bombers and missiles and
thought diplomacy was mere pussyfooting. On the
other hand one can appreciate the far subtler difficulty that the President and the CIA faced, which
was that of not revealing how much they actually
did know – and *how* they knew it – for fear of com-
promising the secret U-2 missions.

In 1956 high-altitude U-2 photography confirmed the CIA's hunch that the Soviets did not

in fact have the large bomber fleet that LeMay feared. The bomber gap simply didn't exist. Similarly, post-Sputnik photo analysis of over-flights by the CIA revealed that the missile gap was just as imaginary even though one of its most influential proponents, the celebrated journalist Joseph Alsop, had himself worked for the agency. Robert McNamara, John F. Kennedy's Secretary of Defense, told the President that he thought the USAF's intelligence analysis at the time of the missile gap controversy was nakedly self-serving and, as with the bomber gap myth, had been primarily designed to wangle the Air Force a bigger budget. This opinion scarcely endeared him to General LeMay, whose intransigence on the subject was starkly revealed less than three years later when he was called to testify at some Defense Budget Hearings. The exchange went as follows:

CHAIRMAN GEORGE H. MAHON: You were talking about the Russians being able to do this and that. As a result of this philosophy of what the Russians could do, a few years ago we developed the bomber gap, and later we were told there was no bomber gap. As a result of this same reasoning as to what the Russians could do we developed the missile gap. ... Now we come along later and everyone says there never was a missile gap. Now, are you by this testimony opening up a so-called megatonnage gap which will never occur and which will be just as phony as the bomber and missile gap?

GENERAL CURTIS LEMAY: That is entirely possible, Mr Chairman.[2]

It is pure *Strangelove*. And so behind the scenes the wrangling went on between the highest levels of command from the White House downwards, as various departments sought budgetary control of runaway military spending while vested interests kept it going by judicious appeals to paranoia. Yet in 1959, in conditions of maximum secrecy at the Lockheed Corporation's works in Burbank, California, one of the world's most brilliant aircraft designers had finally arrived at the design of arguably the most charismatic aircraft ever built. At the time it could only have been achieved in the United States, with that country's ability to fund grand projects and with its vast reserve of technical wizards, materials scientists and remote desert landscapes for secretive testing. Plus, of course, the requisite Cold War paranoia. The paranoia was crucial.

2. U-2

FOLLOWING THE SECOND World War both the British and the Americans rather rested on their laurels where radar research was concerned, unintentionally allowing the Soviet Union to catch up and in some respects to overtake them. However, once Washington had decided its former wartime ally was now definitely an enemy, a motley assortment of American aircraft equipped with cameras began regularly overflying those parts of the Soviet Bloc countries they could reach, taking photographs, listening to the Russian pilots' radio chatter and registering their radar transmissions. At first these suggested the Russians were still using modified Allied equipment left over from the war. But from about 1950 a good few American reconnaissance aircraft simply disappeared, some of which were known to have been shot down. It was clear that with the help of their ever-improving ground-based radar, Russian AAA (anti-aircraft artillery) batteries and early jet fighters were making aerial spying too risky to continue in its present ad hoc form.

In 1951 the Americans reasoned that since the MiG-17, the best Soviet interceptor of the day, struggled to reach a height of 45,000 feet without doing a dive-and-zoom manoeuvre, a reconnaissance aircraft that could easily reach 60,000 feet was required. Coincidentally the USAF badly needed a new jet-powered medium bomber to replace the ageing propeller-driven Douglas B-26 Invader. With nothing home-grown in sight the Americans bought an existing foreign aircraft to build under licence, something they hadn't done since the First World War when they built their own version of the British S.E.5 biplane fighter. Their new purchase was also British: the English Electric Canberra. It was the twin-jet medium bomber the RAF was already flying in a photo reconnaissance version, the PR3. The Canberra entered USAF service in mid-1953 as the Martin B-57 and was itself quickly modified for reconnaissance. By early 1954 several RB-57As were based in Germany. With their greatly enlarged wings these could reach 64,000 feet and

The first Martin RB-57A in stealthy black livery in 1953, when it was still virtually unchanged from the Canberra B.2. Later versions would greatly modify the original British design.

it was generally reckoned this was safely above the range of Russian ground-based radar, let alone of anti-aircraft missiles. Within a year, though, the Soviet MiG-19 entered service, an interceptor that could reliably exceed 50,000 feet, with later versions certain to improve still further. It was obvious that, to be safe, any future photo-reconnaissance aircraft would now need to fly considerably higher. The Air Force's urgency was compounded by increasing losses of their existing reconnaissance aircraft while overflying Iron Curtain frontiers, none of which was capable of going much above 33,000 feet. The best of these was probably the RB-47, a reconnaissance version of SAC's basic long-range jet bomber, the B-47. One of these first overflew the USSR in 1952 and since then three had been lost.

In late 1952 the National Security Agency came into being with a remit that included responsibility for all overflights of 'denied territory', as the Soviet Bloc countries and China would come to be known. The following year the USAF issued an Operational Requirement for an ultra-high-altitude reconnaissance aircraft capable of staying aloft for long overflights of enemy territory. Even as Martin tried different wing shapes and lighter construction to get its RB-57s to fly higher, two other aircraft companies, Fairchild and Bell, were at work on designs to meet the requirement. The Lockheed Corporation soon got wind of this and also began to work on the project. The firm had been building successful aircraft since the 1920s and had produced one of the best and fastest propeller-driven fighters of the Second World War: the twin-boom P-38 Lightning.

A Lockheed Lightning in 1944. Its designer, 'Kelly' Johnson learned much from it about the aerodynamics peculiar to high subsonic speeds on the edge of compressibility.

The Lightning's designer was a talented young engineer named Clarence 'Kelly' Johnson. The son of Swedish immigrants, Johnson was brought up in the wilds of Michigan in conditions of considerable poverty. Fascinated by aircraft and ashamed of his family's penury, he studied his way to the University of Michigan as an aeronautical engineer. There he conducted tests on a model of a new aircraft sent by the Lockheed Corporation, which lacked the university's advanced wind-tunnel facility. Johnson's work on their project impressed the company, who recognised him as an intuitive engineer. As soon as he graduated Lockheed offered him a job. He moved to California and in the early 1940s became one of the design team that created the beautiful Constellation airliner. In 1943, in conditions of great secrecy, 'Kelly' Johnson designed an airframe around a British Halford (later the de Havilland Goblin) turbo-jet engine, itself one of the most closely guarded of wartime secrets. This, the P-80 Shooting Star, became America's first jet fighter in squadron service. In time the P-80 was successfully developed into the more advanced F-94 Starfire fighter as well as the extremely successful and ubiquitous T-33 Shooting Star trainer, scattered examples of which are still flying today as proof of the excellence of Johnson's original design.

Lockheed's factory in Burbank had the capability of working in conditions that during the war were screened quite literally from inquisitive eyes by a vast acreage of camouflaged netting draped over its buildings so as to look from the air like a rugged patch of terrain dotted with trees. This spirited deception had been rigged in case of Japanese raiders who in the event never materi- alised. But the tradition of secrecy continued in the secluded ADP (advanced development proj- ects) area of Lockheed's plant. This was known less formally as the Skunk Works – so named after an illicit still in the syndicated Li'l Abner strip cartoon.

In late 1951 Johnson went to see the war in Korea for himself in order to ask American Air Force pilots what they wanted in a new jet fighter, a most unusual thing for an aircraft designer to do. Returning to Burbank he swiftly designed a stunningly fast interceptor that looked more like a rocket with little razor-sharp wings. Besides being capable of a speed of Mach 2 (some 1,500 mph, depending on altitude)[*] it could reach an altitude of well over 50,000 feet. This was to be the F-104 Starfighter: the first operational aircraft

---

[*] Put crudely, a Mach number cannot be converted into a speed of miles or kilometres per hour without specifying the local air temperature and pressure, which in turn are dependent on altitude. As a rule of thumb, Mach 1 (or the speed of sound in air) is roughly 761 mph at sea level. At 80,000 feet it is about 666 mph, or some 100 mph slower.

Despite the extreme performance of 'Kelly' Johnson's F-104A Starfighter with its tiny razor-sharp wings, the USAF never bought it in quantity. With certain notorious 'sweeteners', however, it sold well abroad.

to fly at twice the speed of sound in level flight. In November 1952 Johnson showed his design to some sympathetic Air Force generals in the Pentagon who clearly thought it a winner. The principle of competition being essential, the USAF formally issued a General Operating Requirement for a replacement for North American Aviation's F-100 Super Sabre, which was strictly a Mach 1 fighter. A mere four months later they plumped for Johnson's design and commissioned Lockheed to produce two prototypes. The first flight of the F-104 prototype took place in February 1954.

In January 1953 President Eisenhower had expressed himself dissatisfied with what little intelligence was being gleaned from the Soviet Bloc. That August an RAF Canberra undertook a daring flight deep into Russia to the missile test range at Kapustin Yar, north of the Caspian, and was very nearly shot down. Even flying above 50,000 feet it was lucky to get home and the shrapnel damage it sustained rendered the photographs it took useless. It was a graphic warning of how capable Russian radar and other defences had become. By then 'Kelly' Johnson was already hard at work on a high-altitude spy plane within the tight security of Lockheed's Skunk Works.

The new aircraft had the working code name CL-282 and he designed it to carry a 600-pound payload of sensors and cameras to a safe 73,000 feet. It would in any case have to fly above 70,000 feet where there was no longer enough moisture in the atmosphere for vapour trails to form and betray the aircraft's presence. It would also need a range of over 4,000 miles as well as being stable enough for vibration-free photography. To save money Johnson based the fuselage on that of his F-104 with its single-jet engine, thus enabling the factory to use the same jigs, although he was now heavily constrained by the need for extreme lightness. This mandated a radical new design. To save weight he stressed the airframe to resist only 2.5g, or two and a half times the force of gravity. This was less than half the official USAF specification at the time for its aircraft of 5.33g. There was no main spar to link both long, slender wings: they and the tail were simply bolted to the fuselage. It looked like a jet-powered glider, an impression enhanced by a complete absence of landing gear, a further weight-saving measure. Johnson's aircraft would take off from a trolley and land slowly on its belly, keeling over on the ground like a glider when it came to rest. Also like a glider the cockpit was unpressurised: the pilot would have to wear a space suit. Altogether, and especially when compared to all the other aircraft of the day designed for either extreme speed or altitude, the CL-282 gave an impression of fragility.

In August 1954 the Soviet Union exploded a hydrogen bomb that the American military immediately feared was more advanced than its own weapon. Once again the US Administration voiced concern over the lack of detailed information about the Soviets' progress. The need for a new spy aircraft was urgent. However, when 'Kelly' Johnson finally submitted his CL-282 design to senior Air Force scrutiny the generals were mostly unimpressed. To them it looked flimsy and unmilitary. Before storming out of the meeting Curtis LeMay told Johnson he was wasting his time: he wasn't interested in a plane that had neither wheels nor guns, as well as only one engine. At the time SAC's notoriously brusque commander may have been distracted by a more immediate concern, for in their May Day flypast that year the Russians had displayed a large new jet bomber, the Myasishchev M-4 ('Bison' in NATO terminology). This again shook the Americans badly. They hadn't known the Soviets had any jet bombers and now assumed they must have entire squadrons of them. They were not to know that several of the handful of Bisons that had overflown Moscow had peeled off once out of sight, scooted round and flown over again to give the impression of an unlimited supply.

A Soviet Myasischev 3M bomber (NATO reporting name 'Bison') photographed from a U.S. Navy aircraft in 1968. Its appearance in 1954 triggered paranoid US press rumours of a nonexistent 'bomber gap'.

In any case the Air Force rejected Johnson's CL-282 in favour of a newly modified high-altitude Martin B-57 and the Bell X-16, a twin-jet design that in the event would never get further than the mock-up stage. However, what neither Johnson nor the USAF knew was that some months earlier the CIA had finally decided the military could no longer be relied on to provide detailed enough information about what was really going on behind the Iron Curtain. This was part of an ongoing battle for control being fought within the intelligence community, as also between it and the three services – each of which had an intelligence wing of its own. Control, of course, also meant large appropriations of funds. Behind-the-scenes disagreement raged as to whether 'intelligence' should refer to that gathered as 'HUMINT' by spooks in trench coats living dangerously or that obtained by 'ELINT' technology such as radio eavesdropping, radar and overflights. The CIA had already sparred with the generals over their estimates of the Soviets' strength in the Korean War (as they would again in Vietnam). It now considered the matter of national security too urgent for further delay. Having been tipped off about Lockheed's secret design some agents paid a call on the Skunk Works and examined Johnson's CL-282 proposal. They quickly decided this was the way forward. Being the CIA they gave the project a code name of their own, AQUATONE. In March 1955 the Agency duly signed a $22.5 million contract with Lockheed for twenty aircraft and a senior CIA officer, Richard Bissell, was put in charge of the project.

Building the aircraft was a Skunk Works project par excellence. The strictest secrecy was enforced from the first, Johnson having completed his design with only twenty-five other engineers involved. This had meanwhile been renamed the U-2, the 'U' standing for utility, a name that gave nothing away. Maybe some of LeMay's criticism prompted a rethink, for Johnson now added bicycle-style landing gear on the aircraft's belly, one wheel behind the other, with a couple of jettisonable outriggers with little wheels near each wingtip (known as 'pogos') for taxiing and take-off.

The blanket secrecy made production of the first few aircraft far from easy: a project of such technological challenge and political implications was always bound to involve a great many people. There was also a subtext of vital importance to the White House. President Eisenhower was eager to keep relations with Moscow on as amicable a footing as possible, which meant that in order to avoid accusations of deliberate violations of Soviet airspace by US military overflights he insisted that any new spy plane had to look like a civilian project. If for any reason one were shot down its fragility, civilian pilot and lack of armament might speak in its own defence. At a pinch it could be disclaimed as an embarrassing gaffe by the private sector.

This merely added to the imperative need for secrecy. There were also delicate matters of demarcation to negotiate. Although AQUATONE was a CIA project the USAF was badly needed for such things as selecting the best pilots to fly the U-2. These would have to be 'civilianised' with a guarantee of reinstatement plus any overdue promotion at the end of their U-2 duties. The Air Force would also be responsible for plotting the missions, supplying up-to-date weather reports and providing operational support such as fuel and servicing wherever the U-2 was based or needed to land in an emergency. It took time to win over high-ranking officers like General LeMay to OILSTONE (as the USAF knew AQUATONE), but once others at the Pentagon saw the aircraft's potential Air Force enthusiasm and support grew.

★

Lockheed's technical requirements were many and varied but whatever happened it remained vital that nothing could ever be traced back to the CIA. In documents and even in speech the U-2s were habitually referred to as 'articles' and their pilots as 'drivers'. Sundry outside contractors were needed to supply or invent such things as ultra-accurate navigation systems, little tyres for the outriggers, pressure suits for the pilots, cameras of strictly defined weight and dimensions with lenses of a certain focal length, as well as sensors of all kinds. Cover stories had to be hurriedly invented. Lockheed ordered altimeters that would register to 80,000 feet from a company whose existing instruments were calibrated to a mere 45,000 feet. To explain this Lockheed claimed they were needed for a rocketry programme. Jet fuel was also a problem because at the low atmospheric pressure of 70,000 feet ordinary fuel would boil and evaporate. The Shell Oil Company had to be brought in to devise something that would remain stable over a wide spectrum of temperatures and pressures. They finally came up with JP-7, a different formulation of the kerosene fuel used in ordinary jet engines. They produced several hundred thousand gallons of it, but only by using petroleum by-products that normally went to make the company's Flit fly spray, temporarily causing a nationwide shortage.[3] That summer flies buzzed unmolested so that spies might fly unscathed.

Testing the aircraft required a place hidden well away from casual observers. It was Richard Bissell who eventually chose Groom Lake in Nevada's Mojave Desert, on the other side of a range of hills from the Atomic Energy Commission's Proving Ground with its growing rash of underground test craters, and all within a securely controlled perimeter known as Area 51. By July 1955 a new airstrip had been built to the fringes of the salt pan and the first aircraft delivered. That August the U-2 made its first flight.

Meanwhile, the Air Force Chief of Staff, Nathan Twining, was lobbying hard for SAC to take charge of the U-2 and put it under the command of General LeMay. It is possible that LeMay had become more reconciled to the design he had so contemptuously dismissed when it was still the CL-282. It is equally likely that he now saw its possibilities at a time when there was no available alternative and wanted Air Force control of this valuable asset. However, President Eisenhower himself put an end to this, adamant that it must remain a civilian project.

As with any aircraft, testing the U-2 prototypes was carried out methodically, gradually working up to the design speed and altitude and with time spent on the ground for modifications. The extreme altitude required of the aircraft brought its own novel difficulties since it was designed for optimum performance at over 70,000 feet and few men had ever flown that high for more than a minute or two. After

'Glamorous Glennis', the Bell X-1 in which Chuck Yeager first exceeded Mach 1. The standing wave patterns in the rocket's supersonic exhaust plume are known as 'shock diamonds'.

all, human space flight would not become a reality for another six years, with Yuri Gagarin's orbital flight in 1961. Back in mid-1955 the upper fringes of the Earth's atmosphere had only ever been examined at any length by unmanned balloons. In May the previous year Major Arthur Murray in the Bell Aircraft Corporation's X-1A rocket aircraft had briefly reached at least 83,500 feet (25,450 metres) and possibly even 90,000 (27,432 metres). With the exception of a handful of Canberra pilots on both sides of the Atlantic there was no one who had yet ventured much beyond 64,000 feet, still less to 73,000 feet while able to remain there for hours at a time.

That summer of 1955, high altitude was to be the U-2's private domain. As the weeks passed the spindly black aircraft was allowed to climb higher and higher in the thermals above Nevada.

★

Not surprisingly, human physiology has evolved to be best adapted to atmospheric pressure at around sea level, with leeway for those living in mountains a few thousand feet higher. As the altitude increases the pressure drops. Depending on the individual, difficulty in breathing can begin at as low as 5,000 feet while a very few can remain conscious without supplementary oxygen even beyond 22,000. But well above that lie two great physiological barriers common to everyone. The first is at around 43,000 feet (13,000 metres). At this height normal breathing of even 100 per cent oxygen will not sustain consciousness and death soon follows. For survival the oxygen must be forced into the lungs under pressure via a mask. This works but is very tiring to sustain for any length of time because it requires exertion to breathe out against the pressure: an unnatural mode of respiration. The second great barrier lies at 63,000 feet (around 19,000 metres). This is the height at which atmospheric pressure is so low that blood at body temperature boils, producing a froth of bubbles in veins and arteries that swiftly kills. It is a matter of raw physics: nobody unprotected survives.

These facts are obviously crucial to the design of high-altitude aircraft. To have built a fully pressurised cockpit into the U-2 would mean paying a heavy penalty in weight and cost. It was far easier to equip the pilot with an astronaut-style helmet and a pressure suit with connectors for external oxygen supply and heating. Even so, the early models of these suits proved awkward and uncomfortable and made the U-2's already small cockpit feel very cramped. Company test pilots were paid to be long-suffering but there were limits to what could be expected of men on long missions over enemy territory needing to remain alert for hours on end. The problem of urination quickly became apparent and an attempt to solve it with a catheter and a collection bag inside the suit was clearly unworkable, inflicting unnecessary discomfort on the pilot and the longer-term possibility of infection. By that autumn a condom-like collection device leading to an external bag proved just about manageable.

Already it was clear that being a U-2 pilot was not always going to be a lot of fun once the lordly panoramic gaze had lost its novelty. Apart from having to eat a low-bulk, high-protein diet in the twelve hours before a mission, most pilots instinctively curbed their fluid intake and thirst became a real problem. A little self-sealing hole in the face mask allowed water and food concentrates to be sucked through a plastic tube, but even so it was common for pilots to lose up to six pounds of body weight on an eight-hour mission. Before each flight pilots purged any nitrogen in their bloodstream by breathing pure oxygen for an hour and a half. The idea of this 'pre-breathing' was to reduce any chance of their getting the bends if nitrogen came out of solution under low pressure and formed bubbles in their blood.

But in addition to the physiological problems of venturing so high there were those posed by the U-2 itself, which proved a very tricky aircraft to fly. Being so light, it could take off at an impressively steep angle, but from the first it proved difficult to land. The pilot would make his approach normally and flare to touch down, but instead of settling on the runway the aircraft tended to float on the cushion of air just above it: the so-called 'ground effect' that increases lift and reduces drag. The pilot's immediate downward view from the cockpit was anyway limited and it was hard for him to judge exactly how high up he was. An accurate and gentle touchdown was essential given the airframe's fragility: the single main landing gear was on a short leg beneath the aircraft's belly with a little tailwheel behind. A method was devised which involved a chase car waiting by the runway threshold and then following the U-2, talking the pilot down via radio through the last few feet of his descent. Other speeding cars would then converge on the aircraft as it finished its run and ground crews would hurry to keep the wings level while the pogo legs that had fallen off after take-off were reattached so the 'Dragon Lady' (as the aircraft was nicknamed) could taxi back to the ramp.

Yet this was easy compared with the task that faced the pilot at high altitude. Having been hand-picked and laboriously vetted, the first batch of USAF pilots had been sent to Groom Lake (soon known to them as 'the Area', 'the Ranch' or just 'the Sandpile') to learn how to fly the aircraft. They were the cream of the Air Force's fast jet jockeys and brim-full of the Right Stuff. The first thing they had to unlearn was their instinctive desire in any aircraft to do loops and barrel rolls and pull so much g in high-speed turns that they were on the edge of blacking out. The U-2 was a *slow* aircraft compared with what they were used to: a combination of glider and jet with wings that provided immense lift but were very fragile. Not only were they merely bolted to the fuselage but tanks within them carried all the fuel supply. It would be all too easy to tear them off with rough treatment. As noted earlier, the design was optimised for an altitude of 73,000 feet where the air is extremely thin, and it was firmly dinned into the pilots that at sea level the never-exceed speed was limited to a mere 190 kt (219 mph) and 150 kt if there was even the slightest turbulence.

But the real challenge lay nearly fourteen miles up, where a nasty aerodynamic trap lay in wait. The true air speed (TAS, rather than the indicated air speed – IAS – on the pilot's instrument panel) at which Mach 1 is reached decreases the higher one goes. Up there at the U-2's operational altitude the never-exceed speed was Mach 0.8: at that altitude equivalent to 394 kt (454 mph). Any faster and the aircraft could shed its wings despite the atmosphere's thinness. The explanation for this lay in the peculiarities of airflow over flying surfaces, whose smoothness starts to break up into turbulence as an aircraft approaches Mach 1. This causes buffeting that can be severe enough for an aircraft to come apart in the air, as sometimes happened in the early days of fast jets. To avoid this, U-2 pilots had to be ever-alert not to let their speed rise even a fraction beyond the IAS that gave 394 kt true.

But there was also a lower jaw to this trap, which was that if they let their speed *fall* too much the aircraft would stall in the thin air, the wings suddenly losing all lift and the aircraft dropping with enough stresses and strains on the flying surfaces to tear off wings or tail. At maximum altitude the speed difference between these two traps was a mere six knots. This made even the most gentle turn, with the possibility of the lower wing stalling and the upper going supersonic, a matter of considerable skill. Thus caught in the six-knot strait between the Scylla of high-speed buffet and the Charybdis of low-speed stall the U-2 pilot dared never relax since his aircraft was always approaching the point of falling out of the sky in pieces. When these two critical speeds were plotted on a graph, the angle where they intersected came to be known, with typical aviators' black humour, as 'Coffin Corner'.

And so, over the months, the Dragon Lady was gradually tamed high above the barren mountains and salt pans of remote Nevada. At her zenith she left no contrail and from the ground was invisible to the human eye. Yet sometimes when the sun caught her polished wings in the cloudless blue sky above the desert someone in a ranch or township far away might glimpse a tiny flash and stories of UFOs began increasingly to circulate. By the New Year of 1956 those in the USAF hierarchy who knew of her existence had become true converts to her spying potential. Yet in his heart 'Kelly' Johnson had little confidence that his creation would remain safe for long from Soviet radar and even missiles, an apprehension shared by AQUATONE's director, the senior CIA agent Richard Bissell.

The letters RCS now acquired anxious significance. They stood for radar cross-section, a measure of how much of a radar beam's energy an object reflected. Tests soon showed that the Dragon Lady altogether lacked stealth. Various measures to reduce her RCS would be tried, including different paints and even a cat's cradle of wires strung about her, but nothing worked reliably. In particular, the wires took the edge off the U-2's performance, which was unpopular with the pilots, who referred to such aircraft as 'dirty birds'. The first U-2 spy operations began in the summer of 1956 and by

1957 both Bissell and Johnson were hazarding a guess that the only way to make a reconnaissance aircraft safe would be to increase its operating altitude and give it supersonic speed such that, even if it were detected by radar, there would not be enough time for the information to be relayed to a SAM site, for the missile to be fired and for it to catch up with the intruder before running out of fuel. This argued the need to fly at a speed of at least Mach 3. Clearly this demanded an entirely new type of aircraft.

Such speeds, though extraordinary at the time, were not inconceivable. In September 1956 a pilot named Mel Apt was air-launched in a rocket-powered Bell X-2 from a B-50 mother ship. At a height of 65,500 feet (20,000 metres) he just touched a record Mach 3.2, or a fraction over 2,000 mph (3,360 kph), before losing control. He ejected successfully, but his parachute never deployed and he hit the ground still strapped in his seat. Later that month his fellow test pilot Ivan Kincheloe took a second X-2 to a record height of 126,200 feet (38,466 metres). But X-2s were essentially manned rockets with wings, with a flight duration of minutes. Any spy plane worthy

The rocket-powered Bell X-2 after being dropped by its B-50 mother ship. In 1956 Mel Apt's X-2 reached a speed of Mach 3.2 before he lost control and died when his parachute failed.

of the name had to be able to carry out missions stretching to eight hours or more.

★

Meanwhile, things remained uncertain for the U-2 on the political front. At the Geneva Summit in July 1955 Eisenhower had made Khrushchev an extraordinary 'Open Skies' offer that would give the Russians airfield facilities in the US from which to take aerial photographs of North America in exchange for allowing Americans to do the same thing in the USSR. What Curtis LeMay must have thought of this offer is best left to the imagination. Needless to say, Khrushchev refused. Now, a year later, it was not just 'Kelly' Johnson who was worried that the latest Soviet radars might be able to track a U-2 at 72,000 feet: so, too, were plenty of US officials including Eisenhower himself. The final agreed cover story for AQUATONE was that if a U-2 and its 'civilian' pilot ever came down on the wrong side of the Iron Curtain it would be claimed that he was doing innocent upper-atmosphere meteorological research. Against the background of deepening Cold War mistrust it must have struck the White House as a painfully feeble refuge.

A U-2 had already made a successful and revealing excursion above East Germany and Poland when, in July 1956, Eisenhower gave his reluctant permission for ten more overflights. Almost immediately these yielded valuable information. Flying out of Wiesbaden, the pilots ventured as far east as Minsk, Kiev and the Crimea. When the rolls of film they brought back were developed, the interpreters could just make out midge-like MiG-15s and -17s falling away far below. This told them that the Dragon Ladies were safe for the moment from Russian interceptors, but not from the radars that had obviously detected them far enough away to vector in the jet fighters. Very soon the myth of the bomber gap had been debunked, much to the relief of the US Administration. This highly classified news must have come as a mixed blessing to a select few SAC generals like LeMay, for the myth had been a useful bargaining chip. However, its debunking could not be announced to the press without making it obvious that overflights must be taking place. Even though the Soviets knew this perfectly well and were complaining loudly, the American public was not allowed to know. That this was primarily a CIA project was a secret that had to be kept at all costs.

The information the U-2s were bringing back was vital to the American military and the Pentagon clamoured for more overflights. These were soon being flown from Adana, Turkey, as well as from Germany. During the Suez Crisis in late 1956, the U-2s out of Turkey were deployed to see exactly what the British and French forces were up to, showing that they were just as useful for monitoring a war in real time as they were for taking pictures of static objects such as missile sites and airfields. Yet a new generation of Soviet jet fighters like the MiG-19 and MiG-21 was steadily becoming more of a threat and, towards the end of 1957, a MiG-19 actually fired its three 30mm cannon at a U-2, albeit ineffectually. Anything that could be done to avoid detection was tried. Ideally, the U-2s would reach an altitude of over 60,000 feet before crossing the Iron Curtain so as to avoid the betraying contrails they left lower down. The aircraft's underside was also painted dark blue to make it less visible against the deeper blue of the stratosphere, but the penalty for this was the loss of 250 feet in altitude since every pound of paint cost a foot of height: a graphic illustration of the fine tolerances that governed flight at such rarefied levels.

The Russians' launch of the world's first satellite, Sputnik, in October 1957 was devastating to American morale and a new panic, that of a missile gap, took hold. By now the US and the UK were sharing the interpretation of much of the data being brought back by the U-2s and early in 1958, in conditions of hermetic secrecy, a group of RAF pilots was recruited to fly U-2 missions. This was at a time when Eisenhower had placed one of his frequent embargoes on US overflights of Soviet territory. The British were trained in Nevada, one being killed when his aircraft apparently disintegrated at altitude, a probable victim of 'Coffin Corner'. The following year the pilots were posted to the CIA's 'Detachment B' at İncirlik, Turkey, and in December the prime minister, Harold Macmillan, authorised two British overflights of the Soviet Union from there. The first went to Kapustin Yar, where the RAF Canberra had nearly come to grief six years earlier, but found no evidence of Inter-Continental Ballistic Missile testing.*

By now the US Army, Navy and CIA doubted the existence of a missile gap although the USAF clung to its belief and generals like LeMay were privately disgusted with Eisenhower for having suspended virtually all American U-2 flights for the previous

---

* The existence of these RAF U-2 flights was only confirmed by one of the participants in 1997, shortly before his death. Despite the release of declassified CIA documents detailing these flights Britain's Ministry of Defence has so far refused to comment.

U-2

sixteen months. What was the point of developing this brilliant technology at great expense if you then held back from using it?

By now there was also a technological challenge to the U-2, but not from the Russians. For some time there had been suggestions that reconnaissance satellites could take the place of vulnerable earthbound aircraft. In 1958 a programme for this, code-named CORONA, was given the go-ahead. This was originally an Air Force programme, but Eisenhower was worried about USAF control of a system it was clearly using to support its own requests for funding. The following year Richard Bissell was put in charge of all the CIA's covert operations, including those of the U-2 and CORONA. The spy satellite programme became operational in mid-1960, just in time for the very incident that Eisenhower, the American high command and 'Kelly' Johnson himself had always dreaded. On 1 May 1960 Francis Gary Powers took off from Peshawar in the U-2 known officially as Article 360 on a long flight across the Soviet Union looking for signs of ICBMs. Maybe it had been calculated that because of the May Day celebrations there would be fewer Soviet fighters in the air. This simply made Powers' lone U-2 all the easier for radar to track and he was detected before he had even crossed the Afghan/ USSR border. A SAM got Powers near Sverdlovsk. He managed to free himself from the wreckage of his cockpit, deploy his parachute and reach the ground safe and sound, if rather bemused. A car bumped across the field towards him. 'The driver got out and helped Powers to his feet. "Are

'Kelly' Johnson and Francis Gary Powers with a U-2C 'Dragon Lady'. The downing of Powers' U-2 in 1960 acutely embarrassed America. After his Russian imprisonment Powers rejoined the USAF and died in 1977.

you OK?" he asked in Russian. Powers just stared at him. "Are you Bulgarian?"' Once they were in the car the driver's companion examined Powers' pistol and traced the letters USA in the dust on the dashboard with a questioning glance. Powers nodded.[4]

Outwardly it was a brilliant coup for Khrushchev, who made the most of publicly displaying the wretched pilot as the story hit the headlines worldwide. However, platitudes about ill winds and silver linings speak eloquently about unforeseen consequences, and these were to afflict both Russians and Americans in quite unexpected ways. A fortnight later the Powers affair backfired for Khrushchev by turning the Paris Summit into a disaster. The Soviet premier had been pinning his hopes on the summit being able to open the way for a far-reaching disarmament conference. He knew that only spending cuts on a grand scale could rescue the USSR's overstretched economy. And thanks to Powers being shot down before he could reach the ICBM site at Plesetsk – the only remaining site about which the CIA had any lingering doubts – the presidential candidate John F. Kennedy was immediately able to claim in his campaign that under Eisenhower the United States was not adequately defended. It also helped that Allen Dulles, the CIA's director at the time, admitted that he couldn't be *absolutely* certain the missile gap did not exist.

Dulles was no doubt being scrupulously truthful. For even as Powers was starring in his own show trial in Moscow on 19 August 1960, the newly launched US satellite CORONA 1 had ejected a capsule of film that was successfully caught in mid-air by a Fairchild Flying Boxcar: the first-ever instance of a mode of retrieval that was to become commonplace. The satellite had made seventeen orbits of the earth. In its seven passes over 'denied territory' it had photographed sixty-four Soviet airfields and identified twenty-six new SAM sites. Its camera could at best resolve objects on the ground measuring 12 x 12 metres, not quite good enough to pick out individual ICBMs with absolute certainty. (A mere two years later CORONA 4's camera had a resolution of 1.5 x 1.5 metres, as good as that of the U-2 despite being at an altitude ten times higher.) All the same, it was pretty clear that the missile gap was as mythical as the bomber gap had been.

Even before the Powers show trial a second American spy aircraft was downed, this time a converted bomber. On 1 July 1960 a MiG-19 shot down a UK-based electronic surveillance RB-47H north of Murmansk. Since Eisenhower's ban on overflights these SAC aircraft were flying daily missions along the borders of the USSR and China, taking long-lens slant photographs. This particular Stratojet had flown from Brize Norton in Oxfordshire and was outside the USSR over international waters. Two of the six American crewmen survived. They were jailed and interrogated for seven months before being released. Much later the MiG's pilot hinted that ever since the U-2 incident the Soviet Air Force had been under enormous internal pressure to prevent any further overflights and he was convinced the American aircraft was headed for a secret naval base that, it turned out, the Americans hadn't even known existed.

Russian technicians had meanwhile converged on Sverdlovsk, gathering up every fragment of Powers' U-2 and its electronic gear. In due course a near-replica U-2 was built as the Beriev S-13 but it never flew because the Soviets were hopeful that their own satellite technology would be more useful. But from examining the cameras, avionics, ejector seat and other kit in Powers' aircraft they did gather a great deal of information.

Back in the United States there were dark mutterings in the press, and probably in the military, that Powers hadn't done the proper thing and committed suicide rather than fall alive into Soviet hands to risk spilling highly sensitive beans under interrogation. When U-2 missions had started in earnest the AQUATONE pilots were offered cyanide capsules known as 'L-pills' to take with them on missions. Far from suicide being mandatory, the CIA instructed its pilots – who were after all civilians – to co-operate with their interrogators in the event of capture. In this they were unlike Air Force aircrew, who under the Geneva Convention were not obliged to give any information other than their name, rank and service number. Most AQUATONE pilots refused the lethal capsules, although some accepted them as grim earnest of the advanced interrogation techniques they were told the enemy might use to extract information if ever they fell into their hands.

Then, in December 1956, a pilot named Carmine Vito flew a mission over Bulgaria. From his habit of carrying lemon drops loose in his flying suit pocket he was known to his friends as 'The Lemon-Drop Kid'. Despite all warnings U-2 aircrew would sometimes risk briefly opening the faceplate of their helmets to pop a sweet or a piece of chocolate into their mouths. One day as Vito was doing his pre-breathing before the mission his assistant slipped an L-pill into his flying suit pocket unaware that it was the pocket in which Vito kept his lemon drops. In due course at 73,000 feet Vito reached for a lemon drop and absent-mindedly found himself sucking on an L-pill. Had he bitten down on it he would have died within seconds high over Bulgaria. As a result of this near-disaster it was realised it would be just as fatal if an L-pill were accidentally broken in the cockpit and the fumes inhaled. All the same, it was not until 1960 that L-pills were withdrawn and replaced with algal-poisoned needles concealed in dollar coins.[5] This was what Powers had been carrying but in the rush of events hadn't used. Some of his countrymen never quite forgave him for that. He was released in February 1962 in exchange for the Soviet spy Rudolph Abel (who had actually been born in Newcastle upon Tyne). It spoke well of the

USAF that it later reinstated Powers and he went to work for Lockheed as a test pilot.

That was the end of U-2 flights over Russia, but the Dragon Lady went on to be very useful in Latin America and the Far East. It was U-2 flights over Cuba that identified the Russian missile sites, leading to the crisis in the autumn of 1962. On 27 October that year Major Rudolf Anderson was shot down and killed in his U-2C by an SA-2 missile. The aircraft's vulnerability was all too obvious, although for the next six years U-2s piloted by Chinese Nationalist pilots out of Taiwan flew more than a hundred missions over mainland China. However, by 1968 the communists' radars and MiG-21s had become too dangerous and men began refusing to fly such suicidal missions and all flights were stopped. Meanwhile, by 1966 'Kelly' Johnson had designed a newer version of the U-2 with more power and much longer wings giving 400 more square feet of area. The increased lift also made 'Coffin Corner' slightly less cramped, now giving pilots a generous twenty knots to play with. Since then the U-2 has been further modified, nearly out of all recognition. Nevertheless, today's all-black U-2S and NASA's all-white ER-2 still bear a visible resemblance to the prototype that had first climbed steeply into the shimmering air above Groom Lake more than sixty years earlier.

3. OXCART

B ACK IN 1955, well before the first U-2 prototype had lifted off the airstrip at Groom Lake, the USAF was chafing at the idea of the first purpose-built American spy plane being managed by the CIA. After all, it was to be flown by seconded Air Force pilots, maintained in its bases by Air Force personnel and facilities, and the information it gathered about Soviet fighters, bombers and missiles would be of prime importance to the Air Force. No doubt behind their opposition there also lay an element of that mistrust – sometimes even contempt – most militaries secretly feel towards civilians, especially those in spooks' clothing. In any case they were determined to have a high-altitude reconnaissance aircraft of their very own and had been smitten by a radical new engine designed by a British engineer named Randolph Rae. Rae called it the Rex-1, and it ran on liquid hydrogen.

Partly by virtue of the extreme secrecy that could be achieved at Lockheed's Skunk Works, and partly because of the faith they had in his advanced design for the F-104, USAF officials asked 'Kelly' Johnson to come up with a design for a liquid hydrogen-fuelled reconnaissance aircraft, the project being code-named SUNTAN.

In early 1956 Johnson duly offered them the CL-400, a Mach 2.5-capable aircraft flying at almost 100,000 feet (30,300 metres), with a range of 2,500 miles (4,000 kilometres) and powered by liquid hydrogen. These figures were not quite good enough for his Air Force clients and he went on to devise a gradually evolving series of CL-400 aircraft. By the time the series reached model numbers 11 and 12 they resembled a twin-engined version of his F-104 Starfighter with podded hydrogen engines. Eventually a design was reached with added ramjets on its wingtips. These remained paper exercises, though, because Johnson soon concluded that Rex-type engines were not really feasible. This was partly because of the hugely expensive logistical problem of providing supplies of supercooled liquid hydrogen at bases across the United States and abroad. It was simply not a practical fuel for daily use by the Air Force. Apart from that, though, Johnson found he couldn't build sufficient liquid hydrogen tankage into a fuselage slender enough to reach Mach 2.5 while also being thickly insulated to keep the hydrogen liquid. So Rae's idea was dropped, although work that stemmed from it eventually went into the Saturn V rocket that first put men on the Moon.

Thus SUNTAN came to an end. However, Richard Bissell and other senior CIA officers encouraged Johnson to work on how to reduce a high-flying aircraft's visibility to radar. The U-2's RCS seemed intractably high, although this factor had hardly been considered when Johnson designed the aircraft. Now, however, any completely new design for a high-altitude Mach 3 aircraft would need to take into account Russian radars' increasing ability to detect intruders at altitude and even beyond the Soviet Union's borders.

By 1958 Johnson was hard at work on a series of new designs that he prefixed in his logbook with the letter 'A' standing for 'Archangel' (a Skunk Works nickname for the U-2 having been 'Angel'). Throughout that summer he participated in various high-level meetings with a panel that

ARCHANGEL 2
SEPTEMBER 1958

Length:	129.17 ft	Zero Fuel Weight:	54,000 lbs	Cruise Mach:	3.2
Span:	76.68 ft	Fuel Weight:	81,000 lbs	Cruise Alt:	94 -105 kft
Height:	27.92 ft	Takeoff Gross:	135,000 lbs	Radius:	2,000 NM

75" Dia Ramjets Burning HEF
(Lit @ Mach 0.95, 36,000 ft)

Reduced Wing Sweep
Compared to A-1

Two J58 Turbojets With AB Burning JP-150
(Moved Further Outboard for Bending Relief)

A Skunk Works study for Archangel 2. The wingtip ramjets were briefly favoured by designers in the Soviet Union, France and Britain but were dropped as being better suited to small Mach 3 – Mach 6 missiles.

included Edwin Land, the inventor of the Polaroid camera. Various ideas were discussed, including one from the US Navy for a vast ramjet-powered rubber aircraft 125 feet long, fifteen feet in diameter and designed for an altitude of 150,000 feet (45,000 metres or over twenty-eight miles high). It was to be carried there by a balloon that would need to be a mile in diameter. In a sardonic note in his logbook Johnson observed, 'As of today, it looks like the rubber blimp would have a radius of operation of 52 miles.'[6] The panicky climate of the Cold War could undoubtedly propel Jet Age thinking into wild and woolly realms.

Johnson himself was still considering ramjets for the latest of his 'A' designs but he was also in close communication with Pratt & Whitney over a possible successor to their well-tried J57 jet engine that was currently powering the U-2 and other US aircraft. Ramjets had distinct drawbacks, the main problem being that unlike ordinary turbojets they needed to be travelling at speed before sufficient air was forced into them to make them work. Consequently, any ramjet-powered aircraft and missiles would have to be air-launched from another aircraft or else be brought up to speed by a rocket booster.

It is worth noting that back in 1954 the Soviet designer Pavel Tsybin had been working on a ramjet-powered high-altitude nuclear bomber that could be dropped from a mother ship. In its planform, or outline when viewed from above, the Tsybin RSR bore a considerable resemblance to Johnson's A-2 model which it anticipated. But then so too did the contemporary high-speed reconnaissance designs of several French and British aero companies (Bristol's Type 188 of 1953 and the Avro 730, for instance). They were examples of convergent evolution, with first-rate designers working independently and in great secrecy at the limits of known aerodynamics and engine power. It was hardly surprising that their designs often resembled each other and were sometimes nearly identical, the same problems having led to much the same solutions.

In late 1958, following the demise of the Air Force's SUNTAN project and over two years after the first U-2 overflight, President Eisenhower approved a feasibility study for a new reconnaissance aircraft. It was given the code name GUSTO and Johnson's Skunk Works team intensified their work. Convair/General Dynamics had proposed a well-received idea for a 'Super Hustler' version of their B-58 Mach 2-capable delta jet bomber that would air-launch a smaller ramjet-powered vehicle. Johnson had meanwhile finally switched his attention from ramjets to Pratt & Whitney's powerful new J58 engine that had originally been designed for a jet flying boat for the Navy and which he hoped could be modified for extended cruise at Mach 3.2.

The prototype of Convair's Mach-2 'Hustler' bomber at its roll-out in 1956. Carrying up to five nuclear weapons, the B-58 was tricky to fly and had a take-off speed of over 230 mph.

It was clear to him it was pointless designing a successor to the U-2 that might have a bare two years' life before the Russian radars and SAMs rendered it obsolete. What was needed was an aeronautical leap into the future with an aircraft so far advanced it would remain untouchable for at least a decade.

By the following summer both companies had finished and submitted complete designs. The radar visibility of Johnson's A-11 was larger than that of Convair's smaller 'parasite' aircraft FISH (standing for First Invisible Super Hustler), which was entirely powered by ramjets. Both designs were rejected. Ramjets were a new and as yet untested technology and anyway there were rumours that the Air Force was very likely to cancel the Super Hustler because they were now pinning their hopes on North American Aviation's futuristic XB-70 'Valkyrie'

North American's high-altitude Mach 3 bomber, the XB-70A-1 'Valkyrie' being readied for its maiden flight in September 1964. Only two Valkyries were built, the second being destroyed after a mid-air collision.

bomber with its six turbojets. This extraordinary
aircraft was pretty much coeval with Johnson's
Archangels, SAC having had exactly the same con-
cerns as the CIA about the dangers of Soviet radar
and ground-to-air missiles and reaching identical
conclusions about the necessity for Mach 3+ speeds
and altitudes of 70,000+ feet. However, although it
would no doubt have been possible to produce a
reconnaissance version of the Valkyrie, it had been
designed as a bomber and would only be able to
manage short dashes at extreme altitude. What was
more, the development of viable intercontinental ballistic missiles now appeared to render even
advanced bombers like the Valkyrie unnecessary,
if not obsolete. Nor would switching that aircraft's
role from high level to low under-the-radar attacks
offer any real answer since SAC's conventional B-52s
could already do that at a fraction of the price. So
in 1961 the XB-70 programme was axed, although
two aircraft were completed for research and flown
from 1964.

Finally, on 29 August 1959, the CIA gave 'Kelly'
Johnson's latest Archangel proposal – variously
designated A.12 or A-12 – the go-ahead. This was
the first 'Blackbird'. Two days later he noted in his

log that he had ordered Skunk Works' Building 82A to begin work on a full-scale mock-up in conditions of maximum secrecy. In almost that same month, and a good year before Soviet intelligence got wind of the A-12, the Mikoyan-Gurevich bureau began designing the MiG-25. It was primarily conceived as an answer to the Valkyrie and would become known to NATO as the 'Foxbat',

The very advanced Russian MiG-25 'Foxbat' was capable of reaching Mach 3 briefly, but at the likely cost of severe engine damage. A formidable interceptor, it nevertheless posed no serious threat to a Blackbird.

a remarkable interceptor also capable of Mach 3 that in its 'R' form would be a high-altitude reconnaissance vehicle. Since it could nearly equal the A-12 for speed in very short bursts it would be much feared in the West. Even in 1973, after the Foxbat had been in service for nine years, the US Air Force Secretary Robert Seamans could still call it 'probably the best interceptor in production today'. However, in terms of range it was certainly no match for the A-12 and its radar-guided missiles would have been incapable of dealing with the A-12's superior speed and ability to jam their homing radar. On the other hand, the A-12 and SR-71 Blackbirds have long since been grounded in museums, whereas the Foxbat and its MiG-31 derivatives are still in service.

★

The A-12 was the definitive version of the Archangel series and, as the first Blackbird, was destined to become a landmark in aviation history, forever to be linked with 'Kelly' Johnson. Even disregarding its supreme performance, for its looks alone it has become an icon of aircraft design. Its rear half was basically a rounded-off delta carrying on either side an immense jet engine topped by an inward-canted, squared-off fin. But that was only half this extraordinary design. It was balanced by a slender fuselage stretching out ahead, as long again as the rear half. From both sides of the sharply pointed nose flattened fillets called chines ran back to blend into the delta. Some likened this long forward fuselage to a goose's neck while Johnson himself was reminded of a cobra with its hood flared. Whether one viewed the whole aircraft as marvellously harmonious – even graceful – or as supremely menacing (and possibly both), it was aesthetically a work of demoniacal art. Yet every line, every angle had been determined by aerodynamics and was entirely functional. Like no other aircraft it radiated an aura of pure and vivid energy. Twenty years later Frank Stampf, who had flown for years as a Weapons Systems Officer in the rear seat of an F-4 Phantom, applied to train as the SR-71 Blackbird's equivalent, the Reconnaissance Systems Officer (RSO). By then the single-seat A-12 had morphed into the two-seat SR-71 but in outward respects the two aircraft were practically identical and not an iota of the original A-12's aura had been lost. Stampf described the first time he was allowed to see the beast in its lair at Beale AFB in California:

> I had an uncanny sense of something animate, something alive, in the hunk of titanium that seemed to be eyeing me as much as I was staring at it. What came to mind was being up close to another living creature whose intelligence we sense but don't understand. I paced slowly in front, behind, under and alongside the black beauty that seemed to absorb even what little sunlight made its way through the open door of the hangar. I was unabashedly mesmerized by the experience. That's when I knew in my heart that I wanted to be part of 'The Program' – whatever that meant.[7]

Back in the autumn of 1959 Lockheed's A-12 project was concealed by the code name OXCART, carefully chosen to be misleading by implying something primitive, slow and lumbering. Even this code name was secret enough to be known by only a few people. Years later the engineer Ben Rich, 'Kelly' Johnson's protégé at the Skunk Works who succeeded him as its director, was to describe the almost manic security that surrounded the project:

> The A-12 inhabited the black world for many years. The CIA knew about its development, as did a few people in the Air Force, a few congressmen and, of course, President Eisenhower. Security rivalled the Manhattan Project. Those of us on OXCART never used the name Lockheed; no drawings were stamped; parts were sent to C & J Engineering ('Kelly''s initials) and we had things mailed to post office boxes all over the city. We maintained perimeter security and even swept out our own offices.[8]

This degree of security made it impossible to test the full-size mock-up for its radar profile in the open air at Burbank, so in mid-November 1959 it was taken under armed escort in a specially designed trailer to the desert at Groom Lake and mounted atop a pylon. For eighteen months the A-12's design was exhaustively tested from every conceivable angle, using a variety of different materials and configurations. It was here that the long, gently scalloped chines were added down the sides of the fuselage,

A finless A-12 mounted inverted on a hydraulic pole for radar 'visibility' tests at Groom Lake. It is easy to see why Skunk Works personnel knew the barren landscape of Area 51 as 'the Sandpile'.

as were rounded fairings outboard of each engine nacelle's forward edge. It was found that these curved shapes reduced the entire aircraft's radar return although Johnson was worried they would have an adverse effect on its aerodynamics. In the event he was pleased to discover they added appreciably to the airframe's lift. The twin tail fins were canted fifteen degrees inward and eventually they would be formed of heat-resistant laminated resins.

In fact, the only metal in their final version was the stainless steel joint on which they pivoted.

This anti-radar profiling was pioneering stuff at Lockheed but it would be wrong to think it unique. At much the same time in the early 1960s Boeing were also at work on a top-secret 'stealth' project they named 'Quiet Bird'. Most of the documents relating to it seem to have been destroyed in the 1970s but a few photographs of a half-scale mock-up were discovered and released in 2015, revealing that with its slab-sided fuselage and outwardly canted tail fins it looked extraordinarily like certain reconnaissance drones of half a century later. It was originally designed for the US Army as a study for a scout aircraft; but Boeing must have forgotten that in 1948 inter-service politics had put all jet-powered fixed-wing aircraft under the control of the Air Force. Perhaps this was why 'Quiet Bird' was never developed beyond the mock-up stage for RCS and wind-tunnel testing. Evidently it was too far ahead of its time to interest either the Army or the USAF.

Meanwhile, unknown to all in the West, a Soviet physicist named Pyotr Ufimtsev had published a book in Moscow outlining a mathematical theory that at last made it possible to analyse the complex principles that govern the reflection of lasers from various surfaces, and hence also of radar waves. Apparently the Russian authorities themselves failed to see the theory's applicability to radar and, incredibly, the book was not instantly classified. Yet a whole decade was to pass before it was translated into English in 1971, when it was immediately identified as providing a theoretical basis for all successive stealth design, for which it became the bible. This delay made Boeing's achievement with 'Quiet Bird' eight or nine years earlier even more astonishing.

But reducing the A-12's radar profile at a time when Ufimtsev's book was still unknown in the West and computers were clumsy and severely limited was extremely difficult. Despite the extreme complexity of the mathematics Johnson's Skunk Works engineers, working in teams, used slide rules and clunky Friden electro-mechanical calculators for all such number-crunching, as with everything else to do with building the aircraft. This was only one of a dozen difficulties that made the aircraft far and away the most challenging of any built before or since. Its weight, speed, fuel capacity and internal space for the necessary cameras and electronic sensors had all to be calculated to the nearest decimal point. 'We have no performance margins left,' Johnson ruefully confided to his Archangel log on 21 January 1960. 'So this project, instead of being 10 times as hard as anything we have done, is 12 times as hard. This matches the design number and is obviously right.' Nine days later he learned that funding for twelve A-12s had now been approved. He was under no illusions of just how challenging the whole project was, as he later admitted.

> The idea of attaining and staying at Mach 3.2 over long flights was the toughest job the Skunk Works had ever had and the most difficult of my career. Early in the development stage I promised $50 to anyone who could find anything easy to do. I might as well have offered $1,000 because I still have the money.[9]

For a start, the A-12's speed was such that the kinetic heating of the airframe from the air molecules rushing over it would be a critical factor. It was clearly impossible to build this aircraft with the usual steel and aluminium. Its design cruising speed of Mach 3.2 (equivalent to about 2,250 mph – 3,300 feet/second or well over half a mile per second) was faster than a standard Second World War .303 rifle bullet as fired from a Spitfire's machine guns. It was faster than a .30-06 Springfield hunting rifle bullet and of much the same velocity as the 5.56 NATO round from an M-16. Wind-tunnel studies showed that at this speed at 80,000 feet the average skin temperature of the aircraft would be 232°Celsius while parts of the airframe would reach over 530°C. (The afterburner and tailpipes could reach 590°C, the latter glowing white-hot.) Even the inside of the windscreen would be at 121°C and the temperature inside the fuel tanks would be upwards of 150°C, or one and a half times that of boiling water.

For this reason Johnson decided that 85 per cent of his aircraft had to be built of titanium, the remaining 15 per cent being composites. The usual aluminium skin was obviously out of the question since aluminium melts at 661°C and begins to soften well before that. Titanium is as strong as steel but 45 per cent lighter. North American's XB-70 bomber was even then being built of brazed

stainless steel honeycomb with Inconel (a nickel–
chromium superalloy), plus some titanium for a
few high-temperature sections like the jet exhaust
fairings. Over in Europe the Aérospatiale/BAC
Concorde was able to use aluminium since that
aircraft's speed was limited to Mach 2. Johnson's
decision to build his A-12 out of titanium was
momentous. At that time little was known about
it as a material for large structures. Lockheed had
been working on titanium for research purposes
since 1949 and the Douglas Aircraft Company

*The Douglas X-3 'Stiletto' at Edwards AFB in
1952. With its stub-winged futuristic design it was
dangerous and barely airworthy. Even once aloft it
performed disappointingly.*

had pioneered its limited use in aircraft with their highly futuristic but grossly underpowered experimental jet aircraft, the X-3 'Stiletto' that had first flown (poorly) in 1952. But it had never crossed anybody's mind other than Johnson's to use titanium for such things as the huge forgings for his aircraft's landing gear.

The Skunk Works engineers soon discovered just how difficult a task the designer had set them. For a start, titanium was very hard to source in quantity and most of the world's supplies came from Russia. It was merely one of the ironies thrown up by the Cold War that titanium ore should have made its way from Soviet Ukraine to the most secret of all US aircraft projects via an elaborate system of untraceable shipping companies and importers. It all went to the Titanium Metals Corporation which duly supplied Lockheed with sheets of the requisite thickness. Quality control turned out to be critical. Johnson was shocked:

> The first wing section was a catastrophe. When we put it in a 'hot box' to simulate high in-flight temperatures it wrinkled up like an old dishrag. … We produced 6,000 parts, and of them fewer

than ten percent were any good. The material was so brittle that if you dropped a piece on the floor it would shatter.[10]

Eventually they installed their own materials testing that was so rigorous they could trace each sheet back to the mill, know in which direction it had been rolled and whether it had been cut with or against the grain.

For all that titanium is a very tough material it turned out to be sensitive to certain other elements, one of which was cadmium. At the time most workshop tools were cadmium-plated to prevent corrosion. This plating would flake off and 'poison' the titanium, severely weakening it. When eventually the SR-71 went into service with the US Air Force a sergeant on Blackbird maintenance could lose his stripes merely for having cadmium-plated tools in his toolbox, even though all USAF tools were plated. Tons of tools used on the Blackbird flightline at Edwards AFB had to be collected up, loaded into a transport aircraft, flown away and stripped in acid baths before being neutralised and returned to the maintenance sheds. Lead pencils were similarly banned. Even the most innocent substances at the Skunk Works had to be vetted:

> We found that the spot-welds on the wing panels failed very early in their test life when we built the panels in the summer, but if they were built in the winter they would last indefinitely. Analysing all the processes, we discovered that in summer the water supply system for the city of Burbank was loaded with chlorine to reduce algae. When we washed the welds with distilled water there was no problem.[11]

Before that was discovered, an engineer lovingly sluiced down the section of wing on which he had been working with a bucket of fresh tap water and unwittingly caused much damage. Even soap was taboo in the hangar and workshop washrooms for its traces of chlorine. Ironically, any new-born baby given its first bath is far more robustly treated than was this aircraft designed to fly at over three times the speed of sound.

In this and other ways titanium turned out to be a difficult and expensive material. Skunk Works engineers pioneered virtually all the ways of working it, having to invent cutters and drill bits capable of making clean cuts and holes without quickly becoming blunt and generating microscopic cracks. Schedules dragged and costs soared, boosted still further by the painstaking search for lightweight composite materials that wouldn't reflect radar waves but could resist the searing temperatures of high-speed flight while retaining their strength. The CIA chafed at the delays to their aircraft and Johnson had constantly to reassure them that things were progressing as fast as was humanly possible. Yet beyond this pioneering of extreme materials, he and his team were hard up against the fundamental difficulty of all aircraft design: that it is always a trade-off. Change any one parameter and something else will suffer. Lockheed had contractually promised the CIA that the A-12 would meet certain performance figures for speed, altitude, range and the ability to carry a specified weight of cameras and other sensors. All these depended in turn on the power that Pratt & Whitney had promised would be available from their new J58 engine. This, too, was proving difficult to develop and looked like being delayed.

These engines were the foundation for everything else. Apart from driving the A-12 through the sky at phenomenal speed they had also to power hydraulic circuits, fuel pumps and other electrics, the cooling system for the aircrew and various components, avionics such as the autopilot and navigation systems and much else besides, while still leaving enough margin of power that, should one engine fail, the aircraft could still make it to the nearest acceptable runway on the other.

Any power taken from an aero engine other than for just flying will reduce its output and make the aircraft slower, taking longer to perform a mission and hence needing more fuel. This in turn will necessitate bigger fuel tanks, which means a larger aircraft resulting in more drag, requiring more thrust to overcome the drag, more powerful and heavier engines, and so on indefinitely in a vicious circle all too familiar to aero engineers. From long experience Johnson also knew that the power output and fuel consumption figures promised by the manufacturers of a new engine are seldom met, just as he was aware that a new aircraft's weight almost always increases because its customers tend to add various 'afterthoughts' as it is built. This demand to squeeze in 'just one more' piece of kit usually sends its centre of gravity steadily aft, ruining its designed stability.

At a mechanical level the A-12's complexity was daunting. A shaft from each engine drove an electric generator and a pump for fuel circulation as well as two hydraulic pumps, one for the aircraft's flight controls and the other for such things as the landing gear, brakes, nosewheel steering and the 'spikes', or shock cones, that regulated the size of each engine intake. The cooling system so vital to keep the pilot from cooking in his pressure suit in the uninsulated cockpit had a 'food chain' of its own, with the pilot at the top followed by a hierarchy of flight instruments headed by the navigation system, with the cameras and other sensitive equipment close behind. Cooling the cameras was a particular nightmare since big forty-eight-inch focal-length lenses and sensitive film needed to be kept at as constant a temperature as possible. Yet the range of temperatures from which they had to be protected was huge. At cruise speed the skin around the camera bays would reach 232°C; on the ground at Groom Lake it might be thirty-eight degrees; whereas when the aircraft descended to

25,000 feet for air-to-air refuelling the outside temperature could be *minus* forty-three degrees.

Such temperatures naturally caused the airframe to expand and contract considerably, which is why Johnson designed the A-12's wings with their characteristic fore-and-aft skin corrugations that allowed for this. Great ingenuity also went into devising a way of attaching the wings to their spars. Merely riveting them together was futile since it wouldn't allow for necessary movement.

The fuel system had equally complex requirements. The long 'gooseneck' fuselage forward of the delta wing was almost entirely filled from behind the cockpit with six fuel tanks (the chines on either side being mainly crammed with 'black boxes' of one sort or another). These tanks were all interconnected and as the fuel was used up a system of pumps would automatically transfer fuel between them so as to preserve the aircraft's trim. The fuel in the tanks would itself function as a heat sink, acting as a coolant for even hotter components. Since it would reach at least 170°C at cruise speed the space in the emptying tanks had to be filled with inert nitrogen under pressure. This was to prevent any build-up of potentially explosive vapour but also to stop the tanks collapsing under the increased atmospheric pressure when the aircraft descended. This would be one more thing for the pilot to remember: if he came down too fast the flow of nitrogen might not be able to keep up, in which case low tank pressure warning lights would come on in the cockpit. As for the fuel itself, this would once again have to be the U-2's JP-7 with its ultra-high boiling point. In this, as in many other ways, the Skunk Works' prior experience with the U-2 proved invaluable in building the A-12 since both aircraft shared certain highly specific problems posed by high-altitude flying.

In addition to the special fuel, completely new hydraulic fluids and lubricating oils had to be invented that would not only work efficiently at 300°C and above but also remain fluid when ambient temperatures dropped well below freezing. Sealants for the fuel and hydraulic systems that would remain effective over a similarly wide range of temperatures also had to be devised. The A-12's vital onboard cameras had their own range of problems. Because of the restrictions on shape, size and weight new cameras had to be designed from scratch to suit the CIA's requirements for image resolution and the width of the swathe of ground to be covered along the aircraft's track. Three different systems were eventually bought. These had to be thermally protected, and since the least vibration would blur the image the camera mountings had somehow to be isolated from any flexing or buffeting of the airframe. One of the items that took longest to devise was the pane of glass through which each of the lenses peered. This had to remain optically perfect at an exterior temperature of 288°C and an interior of sixty-six degrees. This nearly impossible requirement took the Corning Glass Works nearly three years to solve satisfactorily and alone cost $2 million. The special quartz glass they invented needed to be fused to its metal frame using high-frequency sound: yet another brand-new engineering technique demanded by this most exacting aircraft.

The A-12's landing gear presented unprece-dented difficulties in that the tyres had to be able to withstand the heat-soak of Mach 3 flight for hours at a stretch while still remaining inflated with nitro-gen at 425 psi. After much work B. F. Goodrich came up with the right materials for a tyre good for roughly fifteen take-offs and landings at a cost of

$2,300 per tyre (at current values $18,634 or about £15,000 each. The A-12 had eight tyres.)

In short, every one of the A-12's myriad components had to be rethought as though from scratch. There was no borrowing of ready-made parts, as with the U-2's F-104-based fuselage. Everything had to be freshly designed and made, weighed, measured, double-checked and tested to destruction over and over again. It all had to be done down to that last proverbial nut and bolt which, perhaps fatally but invisibly weakened by having been tightened with a cadmium-coated spanner, might fail at altitude and dissolve both aircraft and pilot into an instant rain of fragments.

★

By March 1961 Johnson was having to tell the CIA's Richard Bissell: 'Schedules are in jeopardy on two fronts. One is the assembly of the wing and the other is in satisfactory development of the engine. Our evaluation shows that each of these programs is from three to four months behind the current schedule.' Consequently he estimated the date of the first flight would have to be put back from

30 August to 1 December. Bissell was plainly not amused:

> This news is extremely shocking on top of our previous slippage from May to August and my understanding as of our meeting 19 December that the titanium extrusion problems were essentially overcome. I trust this is the last of such disappointments short of a severe earthquake in Burbank.[12]

This was harsh, given that developing the new J58 engine was Pratt & Whitney's responsibility. On 10 July Johnson confided to his log:

> Having a horrible time building this first airplane and we are stopped on the second by a change in the design of the radar configuration of the chines. Have shop meetings often – about three times a week – but it's hard to drive a willing horse. Everyone on edge connected with the production of the A-12 airplane and we still have a long, long way to go. I told Courtlandt Gross*

* Courtlandt Gross was Lockheed's Chairman at the time. He, his wife and his housekeeper would be found shot to

and Dan Haughton* how tough our problems are, with no under-estimation on my part of the extreme danger we will encounter in flying this revolutionary airplane. And told them some of the steps we are taking to minimize these dangers.[13]

Almost a year earlier, work had started out at Groom Lake to upgrade the old U-2 facility for the A-12. It was a major undertaking. A hundred former Navy buildings including three hangars were dismantled, trucked into the Nevada desert and re-erected. The existing 5,000-foot runway was rebuilt and lengthened to 8,500 feet. Johnson specified that it should not be a normal Air Force-type runway with expansion joints every twenty-five feet because these could set up destructive mechanical resonance in an aircraft landing and taking off at the A-12's speeds. As the first article's completion neared, Johnson realised the aircraft would be ready before its engines and took the precaution of fitting it with two of the less powerful J75s (bigger

death in his Pennsylvania mansion in July 1982.
* Daniel J. Haughton took over from Courtlandt Gross as Lockheed's Chairman in 1967. He died in 1987.

brothers of the U-2's J57) so at least they could make a start with flight testing. He was not over-impressed with Pratt & Whitney's progress with the J58 and after a meeting with company officials wrote, 'Their troubles are desperate. It is almost unbelievable that they could have gotten this far with the engine without uncovering basic problems which have been normal in every jet engine I have ever worked with. Prospect of an early flight engine is dismal...'[14]

In early 1962 the first A-12 – now known as Article 121 – was carefully packed into the trailer that had been used to transport the full-sized mock-up and slowly driven under armed guard to Groom Lake where it was reassembled. Finally, the day came when it was ready for its ground test runs. The nickname 'Blackbird' had not yet been coined since Article 121 was not black at all, its bare titanium finish being without paint or markings of any sort. It only acquired its famous sobriquet once the right paint had been formulated: a mixture of ferrite particles in a black plastic binder that reduced the aircraft's radar cross-section and also helped lower the skin temperature slightly. For the moment Article 121 crouched in the hangar, its long metallic nose peering out through the open doors across the Ranch's shimmering desert and salt flats toward the distant range of craggy mountains. After its long gestation it looked impatient to get into the air until the moment when fuelling began, at which point JP-7 simply poured out of every expansion seam in its tanks and on to the hangar floor. Investigation revealed that the sealant had failed to adhere properly to the titanium in sixty-eight separate places. There was nothing for it but to strip the tanks out and reseal them with another compound that turned out to require a complex cycle of curing at various temperatures. This delayed the first flight by yet another month.

The new sealant proved workable rather than ideal, yet nothing much better was ever to be discovered. All the Blackbirds proved somewhat leaky and their hangar floors were always well supplied with drip pans. Over the next thirty years of service this gave rise to a commonly held myth, which was that they leaked so badly it was necessary to refuel them soon after take-off. It is true they nearly always met up with a KC-135Q tanker before climbing to operational altitude

A KC-135 Stratotanker takes off in 1956, visibly a derivative of Boeing's early 707 airliner. In the KC-135Q version this tanker became the Blackbirds' ubiquitous refueling lifeline.

and speed, but that was because they normally took off with a light fuel load. This was partly to save tyre wear and tear and to prevent the brakes overheating when taxiing. But the chief reason was that if an engine failed on take-off with a full load of some thirty-six tons of fuel the chances of bringing off an emergency landing on a single engine were slender indeed. As a comparison, those thirty-six tons of fuel alone weighed more than an entire Lancaster bomber with a full bomb load. The A-12 was a good illustration of the penalty incrementally paid in fuel the faster an aircraft is required to fly. Blackbirds gulped nearly five tons an hour at cruise speed and altitude which was why, once they were in service overseas, special dumps of JP-7 had to be built for the tankers in such places as Greenland, Alaska, Turkey, Okinawa and the UK.

Once the ground run tests on Article 121 were complete it was time for 'Kelly' Johnson's nominated company test pilot, Lou Schalk, to take it into the air. It was 25 April 1962, still four months short of three years since Johnson had ordered the first A-12 mock-up built. Lou Schalk had been with the OXCART programme for the past two years and knew the aircraft inside out. But taking a new aircraft into the air for the first time – especially one so advanced in terms of both construction and aerodynamics – is always more than a little nerve-racking. This particular aircraft that had consumed so much money and time in the making also embodied fervent hopes for global supremacy in intelligence-gathering. With so much at stake

Article 121, the first A-12, with Louis Schalk at the controls departs Groom Lake on its demonstration flight in front of selected CIA and Lockheed VIPs on April 30 1962.

on that first flight Bill Fox, Skunk Works' Program Manager, never forgot meeting the test pilot that morning:

I walked out to the north side of the hangar where
the bird was sitting with lots going on around it. I
sat down against the hangar wall and Lou Schalk
came over and sat beside me. We joshed a little
and soon I noticed Lou had dozed off so I kept
quiet. Larry Bohannon came over and was about
to talk to Lou and then noticed he was asleep.
He said, 'Gosh, I'd like to talk to him about some
things but I don't want to wake him up.' After a
few minutes Lou snapped back to life and Larry
came back and briefed him on a couple of last-
minute items. I thought, 'That's about as cool a
test pilot as I have ever seen,' and remember it
vividly.[15]

What else but the Right Stuff?

In fact, the first flight was very short and plagued
with handling difficulties. Accompanied by an
F-104 flying 'chase' Schalk never went much above
twenty feet, didn't dare turn and quickly landed
way out beyond the runway's end on the soft pan of
Groom Lake itself. It turned out that the rear tanks
contained what fuel there was and the centre of
gravity was too far aft. It is probable that the flight
engineers hadn't thought Schalk was actually going

to take off but was just going to do fast ground runs. All the same, assuming Schalk knew he was going to get airborne it is odd that he presumably hadn't checked the weights and the CG meter reading. Such things would have been automatic. In any case, over the next couple of days some hurried adjustments and more flights were made before the first 'official' flights in front of cleared bigwigs from the CIA.

This was the big day. Johnson was pleased to see Richard Bissell had come even though he had just resigned from the Agency because of the Bay of Pigs fiasco the preceding year, for which, as head of the CIA's Directorate for Plans, he had been held responsible. These inaugural flights took place on 28 April and the following days. A highly classified Memorandum dated 7 May and addressed to the Director of Central Intelligence, John McCone, described these flights of Article 121 in considerable technical detail but consistently misspelled the pilot's name as 'Louis Chalk', a curiously sloppy error for an intelligence agency reporting on a top-secret programme. Despite the aircraft being fitted provisionally with the less powerful J75 engines, Schalk had by then taken the aircraft to

Mach 1.1 and 40,000 feet and reported it 'felt good in all regimes tested', while Johnson claimed these were 'the smoothest official first flights of any aircraft he had designed and tested'.

One foreseen problem was that of keeping this new high-performance aircraft secret once it was flying. Civilian air controllers throughout the United States were told in no uncertain terms that if their radars picked up an unusually fast or high aircraft they were never to report it by radio but to submit their trackings by written report. The Air Force similarly briefed NORAD, the North American Aerospace Defense Command that maintained a radar early warning system mainly designed to catch any Soviet aircraft or missiles coming into Canada over the North Pole.

Within six weeks the second A-12, Article 122, arrived at the Ranch and was immediately stuck atop the fifty-foot pole for radar tests. 'It was quite an experience to see such an expensive piece of machinery that far up in the air,' Johnson remarked in his 1968 (then classified) history of the OXCART programme, 'but it worked very well.' In mid-June the first J58 engine arrived from Pratt & Whitney and was installed with considerable difficulty. Just

An SA-2 'Guideline' SAM missile on an East German Army transporter. This highly effective weapon brought down Gary Powers over Russia as well as many other American pilots over N. Vietnam.

as Johnson had feared, it proved to have 1,500 pounds less thrust than promised as well as greater fuel consumption. By late December the fifth A-12 had arrived, recent deliveries having included a trainer version with a second cockpit perched up behind the usual one.

Problems with the new engines were concerned principally with the intakes but also with foreign object damage (FOD). Blackbird engines were always critically sensitive to such damage, to the extent that runways were carefully swept and even vacuumed before take-offs and landings. A simple loose nut or piece of gravel shed from the tyres of a maintenance vehicle could be inhaled and cause massively expensive damage. To Johnson's chagrin many of these problems turned out to originate in the Skunk Works itself, with carelessly overlooked small screwdrivers and swarf being left in the intakes as they were assembled, and large FOD awareness notices were soon posted in the works.

Meanwhile, the CIA were increasingly desperate to get their potentially SAM-beating reconnaissance aircraft flying live missions, principally over Cuba to see what the Russians were up to. The shooting down of a U-2 on a Cuban mission in October 1962, killing Major Rudolph Anderson, was another stark reminder of the U-2's vulnerability. It was a further incentive for the Skunk Works teams labouring out in the remote Nevada desert that year to redouble their efforts.

4. FASTER AND HIGHER

B Y DECEMBER 1962 there were two A-12 Blackbirds being flight-tested over Nevada, one with two of the older J75 engines and the other with one J75 and one J58. So far Mach 2 had barely been exceeded and the aircraft had reached a mere 60,000 feet.

Far more obviously spectacular developments had been taking place in another desert some 250 miles to the south-west at Edwards Air Force Base. Ever since Sputnik in 1957 the United States seemed to be playing catch-up in the space race with the Soviet Union. This meant that any record-breaking American rocketry was closely watched and celebrated by the US media. By early 1961 the NASA test pilot Joe Walker had flown the North American X-15 rocket plane to a new record altitude of almost 170,000 feet (thirty-two miles), while his colleague Bob White had taken it to Mach 4.62 (3,074 mph): in other words, twice as high as any future Blackbird and nearly half as fast again. True, the X-15 was a pure research vehicle, air-launched at altitude with a rocket engine that burned for a maximum of two minutes, after which it glided powerless all the way back down to Edwards, where it made a 'dead-stick' landing on skids. But these were eye-catching achievements and were accorded immense publicity. X-15 pilots like Walker and White and Neil Armstrong became national heroes. Within weeks in April 1961 Yuri Gagarin's orbits as the first man in space came as a nasty shock, but Alan Shepard's suborbital trip the following month showed the Americans were catching up. On 25 May President John F. Kennedy made his famous pledge to put an American on the Moon by 1970. By turn Projects Mercury, Gemini and Apollo were to be accorded enormous publicity and practically unlimited funding until Armstrong finally set foot on the lunar surface from Apollo 11 in 1969.

OXCART could hardly have afforded a greater contrast with such nationalist razzmatazz. What was going on in the back of beyond in Area 51 in Nevada remained shrouded in secrecy, a black operation par excellence. It never was concerned with nibbling at the fringes of space in 120-second bites. Its mission was to hoover up intelligence in huge gulps and with maximum stealth. The A-12's pilots would have a more exacting task even than those of the X-15, flying in the Blackbird's version of 'Coffin Corner' at Mach 3+ while operating a whole range of sensors, descending periodically with split-second timing to meet up with a tanker by day or night before regaining altitude and speed, and keeping this up on missions lasting up to eight or more hours. This required pilots of quite exceptional skill.

Even before the A-12 had gone into production at the Skunk Works the selection and training of suitable aircrew had begun. It was noted in Chapter 2 that, as the U-2 programme matured, foreign pilots were often preferred, especially for sorties in the Far East, in the hopes that if they were shot down the fiction could be preserved that such overflights had nothing to do with the US military. With the A-12 and other Blackbirds, considered untouchable by virtue of superior speed and height, there was no such pretence and all the pilots were drawn from the USAF. However, since OXCART was a CIA programme its Air Force pilots needed to be 'civilianised' ('sheepdipped', it was called) for the duration of their secondment.

By most accounts the protracted selection procedure was both demanding and nerve-racking. After extensive background vetting of their service records, likely candidates were discreetly approached by senior officers to see if they would be interested in a 'special duty assignment' flying high-performance aircraft as temporary civilians working for 'an intelligence agency'. If so, they were instructed not to mention this to a soul, not even to their wives, but wait to be called for a week's interviewing as well as lengthy medical tests. So secret was OXCART that there were none of the usual rumours circulating among pilots within the Air Force of 'something going on', certainly nothing that wasn't connected with the space programme. Anybody thus approached was bound to be both flattered and apprehensive, especially since the instinctive credo in all militaries everywhere is 'never volunteer'.

The selection group in the Pentagon had begun their background checks by establishing some basic minimal criteria, the first being that the potential applicant must be a currently qualified and proficient pilot between the ages of twenty-five and forty with a total of at least 2,000 flight hours. Half those hours must have been spent flying one or more of the Air Force's 'Century Series' fast jets (i.e. the F-100 Super Sabre through to the F-106 Delta Dart). Furthermore, because the Blackbird's cockpit was small he had to be under six feet tall and weigh less than 175 pounds. Meeting these requirements at least guaranteed a highly skilled and experienced pilot of moderate size. Meeting minimal personal standards was something else entirely and began with his having to be married, ideally with children. As one successful applicant wrote later:

> They were adamant about this after some problems they had experienced with the previous U-2 program. Their explanation was that the family unit is more socially established, dedicated and dependable. Our wives were also interviewed separately, and psychological evaluations were conducted. Expanded background investigations were run on each wife.[16]

In early 1961, the exaggerated 'regular guy'-ness demanded of USAF officers was to some extent an artefact of Cold War paranoia, itself partly a legacy of the McCarthyism of a decade earlier that had focused on alleged subversion and espionage, particularly in the State Department, the military and even in the CIA itself. The alcoholic senator from Wisconsin had concentrated his witch-hunts under two banners that became popularly known as the 'Red Scare' and the 'Lavender Scare', against communists and homosexuals respectively. To ensure that no closet gay communist would ever climb into the cockpit of a Blackbird no stone was left unturned by the CIA's and military intelligence's professional stone-turners.

Next came the candidate's physical vetting. The fact that he was currently fit to fly the Air Force's fastest and most demanding aircraft was not enough and he had to undergo a full 'astronaut' medical at the Lovelace Clinic in Albuquerque, New Mexico, which was where the first U-2 pilots had also been sent.

The first medical phase lasted five days. ... During those five days they checked out every bodily orifice, X-rayed every part of you from head to toe, flushed you out totally, took samples and measured everything. (I carried a large brown bottle around for 48 hours to collect every drop of urine.) They conducted extensive EKGs and EEGs. I was hydrostatically weighed in a large water tank, ran the bicycle pulmonary functions, and passed other physical stress exercises. I was then flown to the Los Alamos Laboratory in New Mexico to be inserted into the 'body counter', which mapped the fat versus muscle tissue of my body. ... From that date forward I was subjected to many different kinds of personal and professional evaluations. There was the soundproof black box where you had to remain for 12 hours – total darkness, sleepless in Philadelphia – and then the polygraph [the so-called 'lie detector']...[17]

It was during all this that the candidate might have a nasty thought, which was that if one of these advanced examinations were to uncover a latent physical defect that the standard Air Force medicals had not noticed, he might not only be turned down for this mysterious new assignment but also lose his fast jet pilot's status (*never* volunteer...!).

Not having been told otherwise, by the end of the applicant's selection process he was probably assuming he would be offered a job in the space programme. There came the day he learned he was one of a mere handful of successful candidates selected to test and fly a secret new high-performance aircraft for the CIA, and did he want the job? If yes, he and his family would be moved to California where his wife would be told he might be out of touch for days on end, but not what he would be doing or where. Only five men out of the first batch of sixteen applicants made it through to the signing of many fearsome-looking documents. These pledges threatened a fate considerably worse than death if the signatory divulged so much as a whisper of what he was about to do. Only then were hands shaken and backs slapped. In due course the new recruit to this arcane priesthood was flown to Area 51 in a little unmarked liaison aircraft that, had its pilot not broken radio silence at the last moment to transmit the correct code word, would have been summarily shot down by one of the jet interceptors flying circuits nearby in readiness.

Finally, he was permitted to see the aircraft he would be flying as it brooded in its hangar. As with any neophyte who has passed a gruelling initiation ceremony and is finally permitted to enter the holy of holies, no pilot was ever noncommittal about his first walk-round of an aircraft that looked like no other. These were laconic professionals familiar with flying many of the world's fastest and most exotic jets, but, like Frank Stampf who was quoted in the preceding chapter, most were simply awed to silence by what they saw. 'The sun's rays entered the upper hangar windows, illuminating only the nose and the [engine] spikes. As my eyes adjusted to the restricted light I began to take in its sleek length, the massive twin rudders, and its total blackness. A vision I'll never forget.'[18]

Some seven years earlier, the first pilots assigned to the U-2 had been given some ground schooling before they climbed straight in and soloed because there were no simulators or trainers, a situation that was to last fifteen years until the first trainer was built. This resulted in a good many losses of aircraft and pilots, a situation that could not be risked with the vastly more expensive and technically complex Blackbirds. In late 1962, with new A-12s arriving from the Skunk Works and flight testing going ever faster and higher, one of the aircraft was converted into a two-seat trainer that became known ever after as the 'Titanium Goose' (perhaps with a jocular nod towards Howard Hughes' immense and practically flightless flying boat, 'Spruce Goose'). With a second cockpit bulging up behind the forward cockpit, this trainer was the least elegant of the Blackbirds. It also had the less powerful J75 engines throughout its lifetime, which meant it couldn't go much faster than Mach 1.6. However, this was thought less important than offering hands-on practice at flying a Blackbird which, as the Lockheed test pilots were steadily discovering, had its tricky aspects. The Titanium Goose also afforded 'Kelly' Johnson his one and only trip in the revolutionary aircraft he had designed.

The new 'driver' would soon discover why lightning reactions and an inability to panic had been so prized in his various tests. Probably chief among the problems encountered by pilots throughout the life of the Blackbird programme, but very much more frequently in the early years of the A-12, were the huge new engines. The J58 was the most sophisticated and powerful air-breathing jet engine ever built. A single J58 produced as much power as all four of RMS *Queen Mary*'s huge steam turbines: 34,000 pounds of thrust, which can be rather unscientifically translated into 160,000 horsepower (119,312 kW).[19] It was designed to be at its most efficient and economical at a *cruise* speed of Mach 3.2 at altitude with continuous afterburner, sustainable for hours at a stretch. Most of this power was required to accelerate a Blackbird up to its cruise speed, after which the engines could be throttled back. This sort of performance was unheard-of at a time when the tiny handful of aircraft in the world capable of genuine supercruise (i.e. sustained level supersonic flight without afterburners) was limited to exceeding Mach 1 for a matter of minutes before they got low on fuel.

In fact, the Blackbird's top speed was not limited by a lack of power so much as by the temperature of the air arriving at the engine's compressor, a never-exceed maximum of 220°C. But there were problems associated with such critical parameters of engine performance. In particular, there was the famous matter of 'unstarts'. This requires explanation and centres on the design of the engine intakes. When a Blackbird was cruising at Mach 3.2, a counter-intuitive 80 per cent of the thrust was generated by the engine intakes and only 20 per cent by the engine itself. The physics of intake design was so critical for high-speed air-breathing jet aircraft that it was among the best-guarded aviation secrets of the Cold War.

The reason for this has everything to do with shock waves. Below a speed of Mach 1 the air has no difficulty in passing over the wings and other parts of an aircraft. As Mach 1 is reached it no longer has time to flow over the airframe and instead is compressed into shock waves ahead of it. However, turbojet engines (as fitted to modern airliners and military aircraft everywhere) cannot deal with supersonic airflow; the air entering the intake must somehow be slowed before it meets the blades of the compressor. Moreover, the 'superfluous' air piling up in the intake needs to be bled off somehow, in the case of the Blackbird's J58 engines via a unique set of six 'bypass' doors that piped the air past the engine and dumped it into the afterburner's exhaust stream. This injection of unburnt oxygen into the exhaust greatly increased fuel efficiency and in effect made the engine function partly as a ramjet. For this reason the J58 might be more correctly called a turboramjet engine.

The purpose of the conical 'spikes' at the front of the Blackbird's engines was to control the amount and speed of the air entering the intake and also to position two shock waves: a cone-shaped one streaming from the tip of the spike and a so-called 'normal' one that formed just inside the intake. Hydraulically actuated, the spikes could travel forward or back twenty-six inches (sixty-six centimetres). Tolerances were so critical that at any given moment each spike had to be level with the other to within a tenth of an inch. The moment the aircraft reached Mach 1.6 the spikes began to retract to keep the 'normal' supersonic shock wave equally sited in the throats of both intakes with centimetre accuracy. Thus positioned, the air in the intakes was referred to as *started*.

At 80,000 feet, where the air is thin, the spikes automatically retracted to allow maximum air into the engine while still keeping the normal shock wave just inside the intake. If the spike's position was wrong or the airflow into one engine varied slightly – maybe if only because the pilot made too sharp a turn – the shock wave could be expelled from that intake with a kind of violent sneeze that instantly stopped the airflow into the engine, causing a compressor stall and an afterburner flameout. This was an '*unstart*', and the first the pilot knew of it was a tremendous bang and an instant loss of power in that engine, the sudden massive drag causing a fierce roll and yaw towards that side. At Mach 3 speeds the stress on the airframe could be catastrophic. It was certainly no fun for the pilot: in the early days before they were better understood unstarts could be so severe the pilot's helmet sometimes cracked as his head was repeatedly slammed against the canopy.

Worse still, the violent yaw would often upset the airflow into the other engine causing it, too, to unstart. Suddenly the world's fastest air-breathing plane became a fifty-five-ton glider as the pilot, quite likely dazed by the head-banging, struggled to collect his thoughts, pull back both throttles to zero and hit the engines' restart switches. It will be remembered that the A-12's JP-7 fuel was designed not to boil away at altitude. Consequently, it had a very high flashpoint that made it difficult to ignite. In fact, the puddles of JP-7 that gathered on the hangar floor beneath a Blackbird presented so little fire hazard that a lighted cigarette could be dropped into them without the slightest danger.

This very property required a chemical ignition system that relied on triethylborane, or TEB, a substance that ignites on contact with air. When the pilot moved a throttle forward from zero a measured shot of TEB was automatically injected into the engine and this, together with the restart switch, with luck fired it and the afterburner back into life. Various systems would be automatically triggered to 'restart' the inlet and were usually successful. Even though matters steadily improved over the thirty-odd years of Blackbird service, most crews reckoned they would experience an unstart roughly once every three missions. It was just one of those possibilities for which one had to remain ever alert.

★

Back at Burbank in 1960, even before the first A-12 began its tests, 'Kelly' Johnson had worried about the project's runaway costs but could see lucrative possibilities for his unique aircraft in roles other than those of pure reconnaissance. Consequently, he proposed an armed version of it as an interceptor. The Air Force was interested enough to sign a $1 million development contract code-named KEDLOCK. This involved some modification to the A-12. The wings, engine nacelles and the engines themselves remained identical. The aircraft's nose was made slightly deeper to accommodate a second seat for a radar officer. The chines in the extreme nose were cut back to take interception radar sensors. A folding stabiliser beneath the aft fuselage and a little fin under each engine were added to compensate for the slight loss of lateral stability. The result was the AF-12, and the first example of the only three ever built flew from the Ranch in July 1963.

In any case the search for alternative roles for the A-12 was prudent because the downing of Gary Powers' U-2 in 1960 had radically changed the high-altitude spying game. In order to secure Powers' release, Eisenhower had made several concessions to Khrushchev, the principal one being a promise of no more manned overflights of the USSR (a presidential undertaking continued by John F. Kennedy). At a stroke the original main purpose of the A-12 had been annulled, although the inclusion of the word 'manned' had craftily left open the possibility of satellite spying at some

time in the future when the technology was suffi-
ciently developed. In the autumn of 1962 the CIA
latched on to this get-out clause by proposing that
Lockheed design an unmanned ramjet-powered
drone that could be carried piggyback to altitude
on an A-12 and then launched to overfly the USSR
and China. This new project, in which 'Kelly'
Johnson was given a free hand, was code-named
TAGBOARD. The drone itself became known as
the D-21 and a mother ship version of the A-12
as the M-21.

In the early sixties there were thus three different versions of the Blackbird: the original A-12
as contracted by the CIA, the AF-12 (later called
the YF-12A) for the Air Force and the piggyback
drone for the CIA. This last project, TAGBOARD,
remained completely secret to the outside world
until 1977 when the editor of an aviation magazine
spotted seventeen of the completed D-21 drones at
Davis-Monthan AFB's storage centre in the Arizona
desert near Tucson, thanks to a gust of wind having
blown off their tarpaulin covers. Gradually the
story became known. It was yet another narrative of
Skunk Works ingenuity. The drone weighed nearly
five tons and had a steep, chined, wavy-edged delta

wing and a tail fin. It was designed to be mounted on a pylon on the mother ship's back, most of it lying with very little clearance between the M-21's inward-canted fins. It carried a camera and a highly sophisticated star-tracking guidance system that could take it on a predetermined course over a target and then return. The fuel for its ramjet engine gave it a range of 3,000 miles.

Endless wind-tunnel testing exposed equally endless problems and it was not until late December 1964 that the first piggyback combination was able to take off from Groom Lake. Thereafter, nearly two years of test flights and setbacks elapsed as the speed was increased and defects were remedied, and it was not until early March 1966 that the first D-21 was successfully air-launched. However, both the CIA and the Air Force were beginning to lose interest in a programme that had already cost a lot of time and money and was beginning to look less urgent in view of the rapid progress being made in satellite technology.

The end of TAGBOARD effectively came with the fourth launch in late July 1966. Because of the way the drone nestled between the mother ship's twin stabilisers, launching it at speeds up to Mach

3 presented considerable danger to the two-man crew. This particular launch was witnessed and filmed for the first time from the second M-21 mother ship flying chase. The two converted A-12s were flying in formation at Mach 3.3 over the Pacific off Point Mugu, California, when the carrying aircraft released its drone. In an instant the D-21 rolled left and plunged into the mother ship's wing, causing an engine unstart and the aircraft to rear up. At that speed the stress was too much for the airframe and the M-21 broke up in a vast cloud of spraying fuel, the long nose section with the cockpits snapping off and falling separately. It all happened in a split second's filming: the chase aircraft went streaking on ahead at Mach 3 while the wreckage of the other M-21 pretty much stopped in mid-air before falling. Both crewmen in their space suits managed to eject successfully from the tumbling nose section and drifted down into the ocean under their parachutes. The test pilot Bill Park successfully inflated his life raft but the launch operator Ray Torick had broken his arm during ejection and couldn't get into his own raft. He opened his helmet visor to see what he was doing whereupon water slopped into his suit,

rapidly filling it, and he drowned. This was already a recognised problem in the space programme. Almost exactly five years earlier Gus Grissom had nearly drowned when his capsule splashed down, the hatch blew and it began filling with water. He escaped but then his own suit began to fill. Just in time he managed to get into the rescue collar lowered by a helicopter overhead and he was winched to safety.

The idea of launching drones piggyback from a converted Blackbird at Mach 3 was dropped, but the D-21 spy drone itself lingered for some years yet and was adapted for launch from beneath the wing of a B-52 bomber. At the end of a mission the drone would eject a hatch containing the reconnaissance camera and its film, the automatic flight control system and the inertial navigation system. This valuable and highly secret package would descend by parachute while the rest of the craft simply plunged to destruction. That was the theory. In practice the hatches seldom made it safely to earth. Several were lost at sea or mangled by impact with the ground when parachutes failed to deploy properly. TAGBOARD was definitively cancelled in July 1971. It was just another of those slightly wild

In 1943 the P-80 Shooting Star was 'Kelly' Johnson's first jet design for Lockheed and the USAF's first jet combat aircraft. From its fighter versions it was developed into the ubiquitous T-33 trainer.

From the late 1950s the outstanding MiG-21 (known to NATO as 'Fishbed') became the most-produced supersonic interceptor of all time. Variants are still flying in nineteen countries.

The prototype of the U-2A 'Dragon Lady'. Note the tandem landing gear and jettisonable underwing pogo wheels. Variants of this highly successful reconnaissance aircraft are still very much in service.

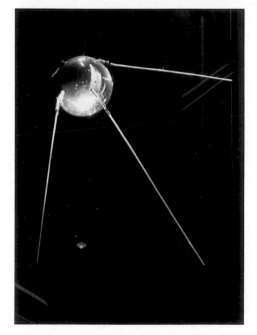

When the USSR sent Sputnik 1, the world's first satellite, into orbit in October 1957 it placed Soviet space technology shockingly in the lead despite being a mere 2-foot sphere that burned up within three months.

An RB-47H at Upper Heyford in the mid-1960s, shortly before the type was retired. The reconnaissance version of the B-47 bomber, it carried a crew of six. A KC-135A tanker is partially visible behind it.

The Avro 730 was proposed as a British Mach 3 high-altitude spy aircraft in the mid-1950s. It visibly shared many of the features of some of 'Kelly' Johnson's contemporaneous Archangel designs but was never built.

The X-15 rocket-powered research aircraft still holds the record for the highest speed ever attained by a manned aircraft, set in 1967 at Mach 6.72 at 102,000 feet.

The Blackbird's cramped and pre-computer-era cockpit where a pressure-suited pilot endured many tense hours at a stretch while constantly monitoring the array of instruments. The yellow and black 'D' ring is for the ejector seat.

NASA's twin-cockpit SR-71B 'Titanium Goose', no. 831, over California's Tehachapi mountains in 1992: in this trainer form perhaps the least elegant of the Blackbirds. Its research programme was to study ways of reducing sonic booms.

A NASA YF-12A in 1975. Note the type's under-engine vertical fins and shortened chine. Twin camera pods and the stainless steel tube have been added for Langley Research Center's 'Coldwall' heat transfer experiment.

One of the Blackbird's massively powerful and complex J58 engines. The thick pipes visible at top right are two of the six by-pass tubes that ducted unburnt air from the compressor into the afterburner.

The Blackbird's M-21 variant carrying a D-21 drone piggyback in 1966. Launching the spy drone at Mach 3 caused at least one fatal accident and the project as a whole was eventually abandoned.

Engineless B-52s being cannibalised or scrapped at Davis-Monthan AFB, Tucson. The 'Boneyard' currently contains some 4,000 aircraft of various vintages but is predicted to shrink as fewer distinct types are produced.

This A-12 (no. 932) flew Black Shield missions out of Okinawa. In June 1968 it and its CIA pilot Jack Weeks disappeared on a flight to check a change of engine. Neither pilot nor aircraft was ever found.

The 'boomer''s view from a KC-135Q as a Blackbird, its square refuelling hatch behind the cockpit open, closes in to take on fuel while he closely watches three dials telling him the boom's precise orientation.

NASA's 831 again, this time over California's Sierra Nevada in 1994. It has just broken from the tanker with a full load of 80,000 pounds of JP-7, as evidenced by the streaks of overflow spillage on the wings.

Two Habus ready to fly, connected to their portable liquid oxygen coolers to prevent overheating in transit to the aircraft. These complex and very expensive pressure suits are in the final preferred orange colour.

A NASA Lockheed ER-2 from the Dryden Flight Research Center landing at Edwards. ER stands for Earth Resources and despite the white livery and wing-mounted pods for scientific payload it is still recognisably a U-2.

Cold War ideas that had seemed good at the time, had created massive engineering problems and brilliant solutions, had cost the taxpayer vast sums and one airman his life. It is not clear now why, if it was possible to launch the drones safely from a subsonic B-52, the CIA and 'Kelly' Johnson had ever thought it made sense to adapt his tri-sonic A-12s as mother ships, with all the structural difficulties and risk entailed. Some seventeen of the drones survive today, either stored at Davis-Monthan AFB or elsewhere, a few being on display at museums in the United States.

The long-range interceptor version of the A-12 ordered by the USAF and known by them as the AF-12 never saw combat. The three that were built spent much of their time trying to solve the aerodynamic problems involved in firing missiles from an aircraft travelling at 2,000 mph. In the meantime the development of the A-12 had continued doggedly at Groom Lake, though not without incident. In May 1963 pilot Kenneth Collins was doing subsonic test runs watched at a safe distance by a chase aircraft, an F-101 Voodoo. Collins was flying slowly and the chase pilot had been instructed to observe the A-12's engines and particularly the afterburners. However, the Blackbird was flying too slowly for the Voodoo, which had a notoriously high stall speed, so Collins sent it away and climbed to 30,000 feet where suddenly, without the least warning, he noticed the altimeter rapidly unwinding although there was no change in the aircraft's attitude. Pushing the throttles forward made no difference and suddenly the aircraft's nose pitched up and it went right over into a flat inverted spin.

Nothing Collins could do with the controls made the slightest difference. The A-12 was upside down, revolving, and dropping like a sack of bricks. It was time to walk. Collins slammed his helmet visor shut, pulled the D-ring between his legs and the sequence worked perfectly: the first-ever ejection from a Blackbird. As the canopy flew off his feet were jerked back from the pedals by cables attached to stirrups on his boots and he was shot earthwards out of the inverted cockpit at an acceleration of some 15 gs. Blackbird ejector seats were designed for use up to the aircraft's maximum altitude and speed, where, if the main parachute were to open first, the sudden deceleration would have killed the pilot instantly. Instead, a little stabilising chute safely slowed him for his seven-minute, twelve-mile descent, the thirty-five-foot main canopy opening only at 15,000 feet. Now, as Collins hung in the air, he was relieved to be safely out of his doomed aircraft and even more relieved when with a jerk his seat separated and the main canopy suddenly spread its great benign mushroom above him. He glimpsed his A-12 disappear upside down behind a range of low desert hills and send up a black column of smoke before he himself made a good landing somewhere in a desert in Utah.

Within minutes he was picked up by three farmhands in a truck who had witnessed the incident. The men offered to take him to the crash site but Collins gave them the official cover story that he had been flying an F-105 Thunderchief with a nuclear bomb on board. Changing their minds with alacrity, they dropped him at the nearest highway patrol office and sped off while Collins made an emergency phone call using prearranged coded phrases. Within a couple of hours engineers and security men had flown in while Groom Lake's flight surgeon picked Collins up and flew him straight to the Lovelace Clinic in Albuquerque. He was unhurt, but after a thorough medical check-up came an even more intense accident investigation that involved Collins submitting to an injection of sodium pentothal (the 'truth serum' of Cold War mythology) to check the details of his account of the accident. This was presumably not because the investigators didn't trust his truthfulness but in order to clear his memory of any instinctive editing or elisions, 'pilot error' usually being the automatic suspicion on these occasions. In the case of Collins's A-12, however, it was later determined that both a pitot tube and a computer had failed so his main instruments had displayed completely erroneous readings.

★

In November 1963, six months after Collins's crash, the A-12 was finally flown at its design speed and altitude. By now everyone security-cleared to go to the Ranch was stunned by the Blackbird. Ben Rich, destined to be 'Kelly' Johnson's successor at the Skunk Works, later described it as 'a wild stallion of an airplane. Everything about it was daunting and hard to tame... so advanced and so awesome that it easily intimidated anyone who dared to come close.'[20] Richard Helms, the Director of Central

Intelligence, watched a midnight take-off. '[T]he blast of flame that sent the black, insect-shaped projectile hurtling across the tarmac made me duck instinctively. It was as if the Devil himself were blasting his way straight from hell.'[21]

With the intensive testing of Blackbirds over an increasingly wide area, to say nothing of incidents like Collins's crash, considerable pressure was growing on the CIA to 'surface' the OXCART programme, as their jargon put it. Better an official, security-edited version of the truth than allowing loony Roswell-style rumours to grow into a tourist attraction. In December 1962 the USAF, under a new programme code-named SENIOR CROWN, had ordered six examples of yet another version of the A-12 as a 'reconnaissance/strike' aircraft, meaning a reconnaissance aircraft able also to carry a tactical nuclear weapon. This would become the SR-71, and by August the following year the Air Force had ordered thirty-one of them from Lockheed. This order, as well as the Air Force's previous order for the three AF-12s, greatly helped Lockheed to cover some of OXCART's development costs. The Air Force was thereby partly funding the CIA's project. At this point the Department of Defense realised that the sums of money being budgeted were bound to reveal OXCART sooner rather than later, and wouldn't it be better to come clean? Furthermore, the Mach 3 technology developed for the various Blackbirds at a cost of some $700 million (about $5.5 billion at present value) had been at public expense. Since this knowledge would also be applicable to much-publicised projects like the XB-70 Valkyrie and Boeing's SST (the stillborn supersonic transport rival to Concorde), ought it not be made available to industry generally? The case for OXCART's continued hermetic secrecy was still further undermined by the latest Soviet computer-controlled radar known to NATO as TALL KING, which could spot an A-12 flying anywhere near the USSR's borders, no matter at what speed or altitude.

A compromise was reached in late February 1964 when President Lyndon Baines Johnson made the following announcement:

The United States has successfully developed an advanced experimental jet aircraft, the A-11, which has been tested in sustained flight at more than 2,000 miles per hour and at altitudes in

excess of 70,000 feet. ... The performance of
the A-11 far exceeds that of any other aircraft in
the world today. ... Several A-11 aircraft are now
being flight-tested at Edwards Air Force Base in
California... to determine their capabilities as
long-range interceptors.

In fact, the bulk of LBJ's speech had been written
for him by 'Kelly' Johnson, deliberately using the
name of an older 'Archangel' version to mislead
Soviet intelligence. The OXCART programme
and the CIA's involvement with the A-12 remained
highly classified; what both Johnsons had cautiously
revealed between them were the Air Force's AF-12s.
This announcement caught the Air Force completely by surprise since there were no Blackbirds of
any description at Edwards. Because the President
could not be revealed as having 'misspoken', two
of the three AF-12s at Groom Lake were hastily
readied, quickly flown to Edwards and pushed
straight into hangars whose doors were then shut.
Still hot from their fast flight, the aircraft promptly
set off the hangars' fire system and tons of water
deluged both Blackbirds and their ground crews.
From now on the aircraft were known by their Air

Force nomenclature of YF-12A. Aircraft spotters dedicated enough to brave Edwards' remote desert location had something to ogle while the CIA's A-12s went on being secretly tested in Nevada.

As for the USAF's thirty-one SR-71s already on order under the SENIOR CROWN programme, President Johnson revealed these five months later as a new, improved version of the YF-12A. According to the script of his speech he was supposed to announce these as 'RS-71's, the letters standing for Reconnaissance Strike, but in a fit of dyslexia he reversed the letters. Air Force officials no doubt groaned but decided it would be too much trouble trying to undo the presidential error and from then on 'SR' stood for Strategic Reconnaissance. The SR-71 version of the Blackbird, always the best-known and most numerous of the type, was overall a little over five feet longer than the A-12. Its larger nose and chines now accommodated a crew of two, a bigger radar, more complex cameras and ELINT sensors. Inevitably there was a penalty for this and at maximum take-off weight the SR-71 was over ten tons heavier than the A-12. Consequently, it flew a little lower than the CIA's single-seat A-12 and the Air Force's three YF-12As, which had operational ceilings above 90,000 feet. On the other hand, with two crew it was obviously better on long, arduous missions for the pilot to be able to concentrate on flying the aircraft while the RSO tucked away in the cockpit behind him could deal with such things as navigation, the precise timing of descents in order to meet up with refuelling tankers, and deploying the cameras and other intelligence-gathering gear.

As soon as President Johnson had made his announcement the Air Force decided to back his claims of the new aircraft's performance by requesting permission to set some world speed and altitude records. They wanted to use their YF-12As, those being the most publicly exposed and suitable of the Blackbirds. (It was obviously impossible to use the A-12s. The ongoing secrecy of OXCART apart, it would have been hard to explain why the CIA needed an air force capable of flying at three times the speed of sound but self-evident that the USAF needed ultra-fast interceptors.) On 1 May 1965 two YF-12As between them set nine new world records, including one for speed over a closed course of 2,070.101 mph and another for sustained altitude at 80,257.65 feet: very much faster and very much higher.

By now the A-12's production had peaked and 8,000 assorted workers were hand-building the aircraft at the rate of one a month. The type was almost ready to be deployed on the intelligence-gathering missions for which it was designed. Meanwhile, testing the new SR-71 with its greater weight and slightly different handling characteristics proceeded apace at Edwards. In the early morning of 25 January 1966 the Lockheed test pilot Bill Weaver with his RSO Jim Zwayer behind him taxied the SR-71 the crews referred to as 'Number Three' out to the end of the runway with Rogers Dry Lake shimmering in the distance.

Bill Weaver released the brakes and lit the afterburners: 68,000 pounds of thrust pushed Number Three into the air. They climbed and accelerated to Mach 3 and cruise-climbed to about 80,000 feet. Approaching a planned turning point over Tucumcari, New Mexico, they entered a right turn with a programmed bank angle of forty degrees. The right engine experienced a violent unstart causing the aircraft to roll uncontrollably to the right but at the same time pitching up. The aircraft turned plan-view against the oncoming airflow. There was no time for thought or action; it was beyond human control. The fuselage broke apart at station 720, the point where the forward fuselage joined the delta portion of the wing. Both crewmembers and their seats were ripped from the structure by forces that tore all the skin off this section.[22]

Weaver was thrown through his seat belt when it malfunctioned, which turned out to have saved his life. His parachute duly brought him down, much bruised but otherwise uninjured, on an endless green prairie. Jim Zwayer's parachute also functioned but his neck had been broken when the aircraft disintegrated and he was already dead when he drifted to earth nearby.

This accident led to an aerodynamic modification in which the SR-71s' nose-cones were tilted up by two degrees, moving the centre of lift slightly forwards. It demonstrated how extremely sensitive Blackbirds were to maintaining a correct centre of gravity. On that fatal day it was later calculated that Number Three's centre of gravity had been several degrees aft of where it ought to have been. Its computer-aided SAS, or stability augmentation system, could cope with minor imbalances far quicker and more accurately than could a human pilot, but no computerised system could deal with the traumatic shock of an engine unstart at three times the speed of sound. Modification of the SR-71s by fractionally raising their noses now meant having to re-fly all the tests, meaning fresh delays to SENIOR CROWN.

★

At Groom Lake, however, the A-12 had by now come to the end of its exhaustive tests. It had reached a speed of Mach 3.3, an altitude of 90,000 feet, and had sustained a speed of Mach 3.2 for seventy-four minutes at a stretch. Some of the last tests had been on its camera systems, and once again one can only marvel at the problems that had been surmounted. Taking photographs of targets from 80,000 feet was not simply a matter of focusing a long-lens camera and pressing the button. For the proper interpretation of any image it was vital to know the aircraft's precise position, and this was long before the first navigation satellites and GPS. By using a combination of aids, mostly relying on immensely sensitive radar, a Blackbird's position over the ground could finally be determined to within five feet and its height to within one foot.

But photographic problems hardly ended there. The aircraft could not always fly precisely level, so the plane of the 70mm film was not absolutely perpendicular, which in turn could lead to distortion. This required accurate correction. Then, of course, there was the problem of the Blackbird's sheer speed. In an exposure time of 1,000th of a second, an aircraft travelling at 3,000 feet/second will have moved three feet and objects on the ground will appear 'smeared' by that much. Thanks to the ingenuity of their manufacturers, the Blackbird's TEOCs (technical objective cameras) had mirrors that moved precisely enough to compensate and keep the image sharp. Some extraordinary results were achieved during the testing of this system. One image showed three men walking across a street in downtown San Francisco, one wearing a hat, one with a nice head of hair and one egg-bald. The photograph was taken at Mach 3 fifteen miles overhead. Another taken from 78,500 feet above Los Angeles – this time at Mach 3.2 – showed a foursome of golfers on a course. 'One of the players was putting. On the photo you could see the flag, the hole, and as incredible as it may seem, you could also see the golf ball.'[23]

On 22 May 1967 the first of three A-12s took off from Groom Lake for deployment at Kadena, Okinawa, in an operation known as BLACK SHIELD. This had come about only after two years' agonised discussion at the highest level. Although this was a CIA operation the Air Force was anxious that the Blackbirds should not overfly China, where Taiwanese U-2 pilots had several times been shot down. They worried that if a Blackbird were shot down, analysis of its ECM equipment would compromise Strategic Air Command's bombers and the Air Force's interceptors that used the same hardware. Officials in both the Department of Defense and the Department of State were also worried about the A-12s being 'surfaced' at Kadena, where they would be seen by all and sundry. In the summer of 1965, during the big build-up of American military forces in South Vietnam, it was proposed that overflights of North Vietnam and other targets in South East Asia would now be of urgent value. However, it was only in August 1966 that President Johnson conceded that the strategic information gained would outweigh the possible risks of losing a Blackbird, although he continued to withhold permission for overflights for a further nine months.

The interesting debating point here, of course, is that if you develop an aircraft in such secrecy and with such advanced equipment it's risky even to deploy, what exactly is its advantage? Eventually permission was given for the A12's deployment to Japan because of the USAF's intelligence that Russian SAMs were being installed in North Vietnam. It was enough. The first A-12 blasted up from Area 51's runway and flew nonstop to Okinawa, touching down at Kadena after a flight lasting a mere six hours and six minutes. Blackbirds were finally about to fly missions they had been designed for.

5. INTO ACTION AT LAST

WELL BEFORE THE first A-12s began arriving at Detachment 1, as Kadena was designated, a menacing financial cloud was already gathering over the CIA's aerial espionage programme and its extraordinary aircraft. Although some ten years had now elapsed since the start of the programme (which by early 1967 had seen the loss in accidents of four Blackbirds), the CIA had still not managed to obtain presidential permission for the A-12's operational use. In May 1967 it had tried to get official sanction to overfly Tallinn, Estonia, to investigate probable SAM sites. Permission refused. Regardless of the aircraft's potential intelligence-collecting value, the US Bureau of the Budget foresaw only the rapidly escalating costs of having to keep the Air Force's growing fleet of SR-71s in the air in addition to the CIA's dozen A-12s. By now 'Kelly' Johnson was also under pressure from Lockheed's management to save money. He considered standing down some of the workforce dedicated to the A-12 and reluctantly began planning storage at Palmdale for his masterpieces.

The sudden order for the deployment of a handful of A-12s to Kadena in May 1967 seemed to come as a reprieve. This Okinawa posting had first been mooted in 1965, the idea being that the Blackbirds would replace the vulnerable U-2s overflying China, and accommodation was hurriedly constructed at Kadena airfield to house the A-12 and tanker crews in a way that would isolate them from the rest of the base. Two years later the Pentagon's overwhelming concern was the deepening morass in Vietnam and the new arrivals would surely have known where they would be most likely to fly their missions. They now took up residence in their new quarters in Building 318, beginning a tradition whereby the elite Blackbird crews modified and decorated their spartan rooms according to personal whim. Security was absolute. Nobody else had access to the building, which existed in a sort of bubble of the Right Stuff magically isolated from the everyday military discipline imposed on lesser ranks.

Other instant traditions sprang up of the sort that characterise special units everywhere. Soon Blackbird pilots and RSOs were instantly identifiable on base by their distinctive 'orange bag' flight suits with the 'Habu' patch sewn on to the left upper arm. This was only given to those who had flown an operational mission and depicted the *habu*, a local Okinawan pit viper that Blackbird fliers adopted as their icon. (The aircraft themselves were sometimes referred to as Habus.) Habus formed aviation's most exclusive community, as they still do. Nobody who wasn't a true, righteous Habu who had flown 'hot' missions at Mach 3 would ever dare wear the badge. It would be as unthinkable as going around pretending to be a Nobel prize-winner, and equally asking for trouble. The Habu motto was a dismissive 'Subsonic is a waste of time'. Their drink of choice was vodka and tonic, known as the 'basic hook' – 'hook' being slang for any alcohol. Any Habu on TDY (temporary duty) to Kadena would lay in copious amounts of both in the bar in his room for riotous off-duty parties. Naturally, anyone on the 'Ops ladder' who might be deployed on a mission in the next forty-eight hours remained scrupulously sober.

The first BLACK SHIELD mission was successfully flown from Kadena over North Vietnam on 31 May 1967 and lasted three hours and thirty-nine minutes. It was looking for possible surface-to-surface ballistic missile sites. For the past eighteen months USAF and US Navy aircraft had been flying appallingly dangerous 'Wild Weasel' missions over Hanoi and elsewhere in North Vietnam. Part of Operation Rolling Thunder, these often suicidal incursions into enemy territory were designed not merely to

An SA-2 missile closing on a USAF F-105D Thunderchief over N. Vietnam. The anti-aircraft defences that bristled around Hanoi, in particular, rendered the 'Thuds'' attacks lethally hazardous.

bomb strategic targets but to bait SAM radars into locking on to the intruder for long enough for the pilot to get a fix on the missile battery. Losses of aircraft and pilots were already heavy (in 1967 alone 362 US aircraft were lost over North Vietnam). On that first BLACK SHIELD mission, and in a mere couple of passes at a safe 80,000 feet, the A-12 was able to photograph seventy of the known 190 SAM sites without detecting a single hostile radar signal aimed at it. This suggested that neither the North Vietnamese nor the Chinese had any idea of the Blackbird's presence. Still looking for evidence of surface-to-surface missiles, similar missions went on until mid-July by which time it was virtually certain that as yet North Vietnam had none.

By then the procedure for such missions had hardened into a ritual that was to continue for as long as Blackbirds were flown over the next twenty years. Every mission was planned and monitored from first to last by the Pentagon's Joint Reconnaissance Center (JRC). Notification was relayed to the relevant detachment – in the present case Kadena – as an 'Alert Notification'. In the detachment there were always three pilots on the 'Ops ladder' – or three crews in the case of the two-seat SR-71s: primary fliers, backup fliers and 'day off'. Immediately on receipt of notification the primary flier was told and his aircraft selected, as was the backup flier with a second aircraft in case the primary flier or his aircraft suddenly went sick. On the evening before the mission both fliers were briefed while the two aircraft were readied. Early next morning there was a final briefing that included the latest weather reports and forecasts and a summary of each aircraft's condition from its crew chief. Two hours before take-off the primary flier had a medical examination, donned his pressure suit and climbed into his Blackbird. If at this late stage there was a mechanical malfunction his mission was aborted and the backup flier and aircraft would go through the same procedure, taking off an hour later. When the SR-71 was deployed its two-man crews always flew together. If one man went sick before a mission their 'primary crew' status dropped back to 'day off'. Some crews flew together for as long as five years.

A typical BLACK SHIELD mission over North Vietnam would last around four hours. It involved the pilot taking off from Kadena, climbing to 26,000 feet to meet up with a tanker and refuelling.

He would then fly to South Vietnam, cross the
DMZ (Demilitarised Zone) into North Vietnam
and make an east–west pass over Hanoi, descend
once more to refuel over Thailand, climb back and
return to North Vietnam to make a west–east pass
over the target area before returning to Kadena. So
great was the Blackbird's speed that a single pass
over North Vietnam would take a mere twelve and
a half minutes, after which it had to turn. Without
exceeding the airframe's g limits and risking an
unstart, the tightest semicircle it could fly while
turning at speed was some 140 miles across, which
meant that overflying China was often unavoidable.
The Blackbird was emphatically not designed for
quick manoeuvres. Fifty tons of aircraft travelling at
3,000 feet/second represents a huge momentum.
Changing direction costs large amounts of energy,
and any expenditure of energy (in the form of
fuel) further cuts down the aircraft's range. Gentle
wide-radius turns were therefore essential from all
points of view.

Once back in Kadena the aircraft's cameras were
unloaded and the film flown to a USAF processing
plant elsewhere in Japan, the idea being to get the
information to army commanders on the ground

in South Vietnam within twenty-four hours at the outside. 'Kelly' Johnson was delighted – though probably not surprised – to hear that a mere six A-12 missions, together adding up to little more than an hour and a quarter spent over North Vietnam, gathered more useful information than had a year's efforts by all previous sources.

However, the Blackbirds' flights were neither undetected nor unopposed for long. That autumn the first missiles were fired at the aircraft, albeit without causing damage. On 30 October Dennis Sullivan flew his A-12 for two passes over North Vietnam. On the first he detected several TALL KING radar contacts. On the return pass his cameras recorded the contrails of at least six missiles. He was at 84,000 feet and travelling at Mach 3.1 and saw three explode. Only after landing was a fragment of metal discovered harmlessly embedded in the underside of his right wing. It was the only time any Blackbird was ever hit by hostile fire in some thirty years of service, even though it was estimated that anything up to a thousand missiles were fired at them at one time or another. The effectiveness of 'Kelly' Johnson's 'faster and higher' defence had been proved to the hilt.

At the end of January 1968 North Korea captured an American naval spy ship, claiming the USS *Pueblo* had deliberately violated its national waters. This became a famous Cold War incident, the crew remaining prisoners for eleven months. BLACK SHIELD missions were immediately flown out of Kadena over North Korea in search of the missing vessel, one of which spotted it in Wonsan harbour. But the A-12's Okinawa deployment was coming to an end. Four months later, on 8 May, an overflight of North Korea turned out to be the very last BLACK SHIELD mission. However, on 4 June Jack Weeks took off from Kadena for an engine check and never returned. He and his aircraft disappeared without trace some 520 miles east of Manila and to this day nobody knows what happened. An unstart leading to catastrophic disintegration seems the likeliest explanation but the Pacific Ocean will no doubt hide the truth for ever.

★

OXCART was now finally halted. Budgetary pressures had proved too much, the government's bean counters not unreasonably questioning the need to maintain two very expensive fleets of Blackbirds, one belonging to the CIA and the other to the USAF. The matter of which type was the better had long been contentious, the CIA quite correctly claiming their A-12s flew higher and had better cameras. The Air Force countered with equal plausibility, pointing out that their two-man SR-71s had better sensors and electronic intelligence gear. The upshot was that back in November 1967 a fly-off exercise named NICE GIRL took place between the two types over a measured course along the Mississippi.

Neither girl having proved conclusively nicer, a decision was taken to stand down the A-12s and mothball them. Even more final was the letter Lockheed received from the Pentagon in February 1968. This confirmed that the Air Force contract to build Blackbirds was now at an end. In its place a new contract was issued for servicing and maintaining the aircraft that had been built. Lockheed was summarily ordered to destroy all the jigs and tooling used to build the A-12, the YF-12 *and* the SR-71, thus officially ending all possibility of further production of Blackbirds in any shape or form. Such sweeping measures were not unknown in the industry either in the USA or the UK. Three years earlier the British Aircraft Corporation had been ordered to do exactly the same with its production line of the now-cancelled TSR-2. Such brutality by decree is always devastating to management, work force and company morale, especially when those jigs and tools represent the outcome of hard-won and ground-breaking knowledge. As the British aeronautical engineer Sir Sydney Camm (who designed the Hawker Hurricane) astutely observed at the time: 'All modern aircraft have four dimensions: span, length, height and politics. TSR-2 simply got the first three right.'[24] Exactly the same might have been said of 'Kelly' Johnson's Blackbirds, and at the Skunk Works it no doubt was.

Eight A-12s were already in storage at Palmdale, California, and the surviving two at Kadena flew back to join them. Only their valuable J58 engines could be cannibalised for the Air Force's fleet of SR-71s now amassing at Beale AFB, California, which was to be the Blackbirds' permanent home base in the continental United States. Otherwise, almost nothing of the A-12s was of use to the Air Force. Even their magnificent Perkin-Elmer cameras were too big for the SR-71's camera compartment. As two CIA historians were to observe, 'Now after only 29 operational missions the most advanced aircraft ever built was to be put out to pasture. The abandonment of OXCART did not result from any shortcomings of the aircraft; the causes lay in fiscal pressures and competition between the reconnaissance programmes of the CIA and the Air Force.'[25]

Such, at any rate, was the Agency historians' view. Yet there was rather more to it than that. The A-12 had from the first been planned as the U-2's successor for gathering tactical and strategic intelligence, but in the event it was only latterly allowed to fulfil that role, frequently thwarted as it had been by presidential edicts banning overflights of the USSR. Yet the fact remains that in most economics-based analyses this brilliant aircraft simply wasn't as serviceable as the old 'Dragon Lady'. It is true the U-2 didn't have the A-12's near-immunity to Soviet missiles, although its new ECM suites made it very much less vulnerable than it had been in Gary Powers' day. But U-2s had a simpler and cheaper quick-response turnaround. A-12 missions were choreographed days ahead in minute detail, full of intricate and expensive logistics, the rendezvous with aerial tankers timed within seconds to take on tons of fuel at exactly specified heights and co-ordinates, and emergency landing places with suitably long runways in friendly territory carefully selected before each mission (a 'land-away' in the jargon). Moreover, the A-12's accurate but immensely complex inertial navigation system (INS) could sometimes take days to programme and stabilise. The sheer complexity of the aircraft's various systems required a large and highly specialised ground crew to work day and night before each mission.

Exactly how useful is an aircraft that can take days to prepare for a sortie when there is another that can be readied within hours by a third as many people at a fraction of the cost? The first U-2s cost less than $1 million each, in contrast to the first A-12s' $20 million. Blackbirds in all forms came and went within thirty years or so, but U-2s are still usefully flying to this day in modern variants after sixty years' service. (In passing, it should be noted that NASA is still flying the final evolution of the old Canberra/Martin B-57, the WB-57F.) This is not accidental. The 'faster and higher' syndrome has always dogged the procurement of hardware in militaries everywhere, and never more so than during the Cold War. Boys in uniform usually want the sexiest – and generally most expensive – toys. Yet it often turns out that the most useful hardware is a cheaper alternative, easier to service, with less performance but available in greater numbers and more speedily. In the Second World War the Allies' Spitfires and Mustangs had the solo glamour factor in spades; but the decisive tide-of-battle-turners were far more likely to be the great fleets of humble C-47 Dakotas dropping troops and supplies. In military matters the workhorse nearly always proves more valuable than the racehorse.

It also was true that by 1967 a good deal of photographic intelligence was achievable from spy satellites without anyone having to worry about presidential embargoes of overflights. The CIA's CORONA satellite project of the late 1950s had by now morphed into a whole series of spy satellites such that in 1967, even as the first A-12s were being deployed to Kadena, President Johnson could declare in a speech, 'Without satellites, I'd be operating by guess. But tonight we know how many missiles the enemy has, and it turned out our guesses were way off. We were doing things we didn't need to do. We were building things we didn't need to build. We were harbouring fears we didn't need to harbour.'[26] Was he thinking of the hugely taxing and expensive Blackbird programme when referring to 'things we didn't need to build'?

Two years later, commenting on a report of the House Armed Services Committee, the American investigative journalist I. F. Stone was to write:

> The truth is that we have spent a trillion dollars since World War II on a gigantic hoax. The US emerged from World War II, as from World War I, virtually unscathed, enormously enriched and – with the atom bomb – immeasurably more powerful than any nation on earth had ever been. The notion that it was in danger of attack from a devastated Soviet Union with 25 million war dead and a generation behind it in industrial development was a wicked fantasy. But this myth has been the mainstay of the military and the war machine.[27]

This was, of course, tendentious. From the beginning of the Vietnam War Stone's well-known left-wing views had been easily dismissed as communist propaganda by the American establishment, whether military or civilian, many believing him to be a Soviet agent. However, once the 1968 Tet Offensive had clearly marked the war as lost in terms of public support, such views as Stone's were reluctantly given increasing credence by people who previously would never have considered them as anything other than treasonous. Thoughtful citizens began endorsing some formerly un-American ideas, suddenly remembering a significant passage in President Eisenhower's Farewell Address to the Nation in January 1961:

> The conjunction of an immense military establishment and a large arms industry is new in the American experience. ... In the councils of government we must guard against the acquisition of unwarranted influence, whether sought or unsought, by the military-industrial complex.

The military-industrial complex. Seven years later many disillusioned Americans took this phrase as suggesting a national conspiracy. What (they asked) was the point of all this vastly expensive weaponry if it couldn't win a war against an enemy wearing rubber sandals made from truck tyres who continued to wheel their dismantled artillery down the Ho Chi Minh Trail on bicycles despite the fiercest and most unremitting bombing campaign that SAC could muster? An ex-military man himself, Eisenhower had seen how the Cold War escalation of American military spending – itself inflated by inter-service rivalries for funds – might, if unchecked, eventually turn the United States into a garrison state and its economy into a slave of rampant militarism.

So, in terms of military effectiveness for dollars spent, and given the rapidly increasing numbers and abilities of American spy satellites by 1967, what had been the true worth of OXCART's short-lived A-12 Blackbird deployment to Kadena? Arguably, the answer probably lay as much in the major advances in technology and know-how that building and flying the aircraft had made necessary as in the undoubtedly valuable military intelligence the A-12s acquired. As the CIA's historians were later to write, these advances were in

aerodynamic design, high-impact plastics, engine performance, cameras, ECMs, pilot life-support

systems, anti-radar devices, use of non-metal-
lic materials for major aircraft assemblies, and
improvements in milling, machining and shap-
ing titanium. In all of these areas [the Blackbird]
pushed back the frontiers of aerospace technology and helped lay the foundation for future
'stealth' research.[28]

In contrast, by the mid-1960s 'Kelly' Johnson's
U-2s had proved overwhelmingly valuable and
cost-effective at fulfilling their original design
function of gathering intelligence. The one and
a quarter million feet of film they had shot (some
250 miles) had enabled intelligence chiefs to
dismiss the bomber gap and later helped confirm
the missile gap as mythical. The same footage had
also established that in pushing forward its nuclear
research programme the USSR had not violated any
of the test-ban treaties then in force, and neither
had it increased its stockpiles of weapons. This
information had greatly strengthened Eisenhower's
(and later Kennedy's) hand when dealing with
Khrushchev, the United States Air Force and the
alarmist leader writers of the American press. Even
OXCART's initial discovery in May–June 1967 that

North Vietnam had no effective radar detection of the A-12s' high-altitude overflights remained true for a mere three or four months. At almost exactly the same moment the Dragon Lady had moved to another theatre and was proving of value in strategic intelligence by monitoring the Arab–Israeli War.

★

By late 1967 all thirty-one SR-71s the Air Force had ordered from Lockheed had been delivered. In view of what has just been said about the A-12 it should be emphasised that in its single year's operations OXCART had in fact gathered a good deal of valuable and life-saving information for the military, while the SR-71s that succeeded it at Kadena and elsewhere went on to produce great quantities of vital intelligence over the following quarter-century. They were highly successful for the rest of the war in Vietnam and in South East Asia generally. By late September 1969 they had flown well over a hundred 'hot' missions out of Kadena. The Blackbirds, their cameras and other sensing equipment proved to be efficient and dependable. Moreover, in answer to their critics they did preserve one clear advantage over satellites in that they could be sent to a particular spot at a moment's notice. Satellites passed overhead every ninety minutes at best; but a Blackbird could obtain multiple swathes of 'take' (in the jargon) from different angles in real time, and nor were their imaging systems as compromised by darkness and cloud cover as were those of the satellites of the day. Apart from which, in May 1972 two SR-71s flew a morale-boosting mission over Hanoi timed to create two sonic booms exactly fifteen seconds apart in a pre-arranged signal to American PoWs in their cages in the 'Hanoi Hilton': not something achievable by satellite.

Indeed, so efficient were the SR-71s, with a single aircraft on a mission able to acquire prodigious amounts of high-quality 'take', that the fleet of thirty-one at Beale AFB found itself severely under-employed. Lockheed's Skunk Works, relieved of the financial burden of producing Blackbirds, had moved on to the next generation, that of genuine stealth aircraft. In late 1970 NASA inquired about the possibility of obtaining an SR-71 for use in their embryonic Space Shuttle programme. Eventually funding was found and an aircraft sold to NASA and in due course it performed much useful research work. But this scarcely improved Lockheed's balance sheet and 'Kelly' Johnson found himself having to mothball five of his precious SR-71s to join the A-12s at Palmdale, citing a 'lack of missions and money'.[29] Over the next two years most Blackbirds that returned from a tour of duty at Kadena went straight into storage at Beale. By late 1973, with the US military engagement in Vietnam virtually at an end, nearly all the remaining Blackbirds were stood down after more than 600 fruitful missions over the war zone.

There was no question that Johnson's remarkable aircraft had been a triumph, performing to specification and even better than anyone other than its designer had secretly dared to hope. Though often fired on, no Blackbird was ever lost to enemy action although a few had been written off by mechanical problems, engine fires and the usual accidents that can afflict any aircraft at any time. What was more, in over thirty years and in all the Blackbird's types there were only ever four fatalities: two back-seat Lockheed engineers and two CIA pilots. This must be an unparalleled record for a high-performance aircraft flying potentially dangerous missions, and is a tribute to 'Kelly' Johnson and the small army of maintenance engineers and tanker aircrews that serviced it.

Meanwhile, a second deployment of Blackbirds outside the US had taken place. This was to RAF Mildenhall, officially known as Det. (for Detachment) 4. For much of the 1970s and 1980s there was a permanent SR-71 presence there with at least two on round-the-clock standby. A TDY posting there was much prized, even though flying sorties in Europe was in some ways a trickier challenge than flying out of Kadena, where long stretches of a mission took place over uncontested empty ocean. In Europe there was a good deal of civil air traffic to avoid, plus so many countries that couldn't be overflown and which at a Blackbird's cruise speed seemed to be packed uncomfortably close to one another. Crews needed to follow religiously the 'Black Line' and timings of their course on the mission map. In those decades Blackbirds also made temporary visits to so-called FOLs (forward operating locations) all over the world, including to Diego Garcia, the USAF base leased from the UK in the Indian Ocean. Indeed, at one time or another they overflew trouble spots on every continent.

In the early part of the 1970s 'Kelly' Johnson had continued to dream up alternative uses for his aircraft in order to justify its value to the Air Force, such as adapting it to drop laser-guided bombs. But the incoming Carter Administration was keen to cut budgets and this and other ideas were to die more or less stillborn. In 1976 the Air Force decided that they could at the very least better some of the speed and altitude records their YF-12As had set some years earlier. SR-71s now established a series of records that stand to this day, notably those of sustained height (85,069 feet or 25,929 metres) and speed in a straight line (2,193.17 mph or 3,530 kph). There was also a famous nonstop flight from Beale AFB in California to RAE Farnborough in which the New York to London stretch took a mere one hour fifty-four minutes and 56.4 seconds. Concorde appeared to dawdle by comparison.

Such speeds could make for memorable missions. Ed Yeilding, the pilot who was to fly the last supersonic SR-71 flight at the aircraft's retirement in 1990, recalled what it was like to fly across the 'terminator' – the demarcation between night and day.

Heading at altitude towards night 'felt as though you were flying into a black wall'. He remembered a particular mission out of Mildenhall to the Arctic, where in winter the terminator runs more east–west than it does north–south. 'Flying that mission, we were surprised that the supersonic portion of our reconnaissance track crossed the terminator six times. In less than an hour's time Steve [Lee] and I had seen three sunsets and three sunrises.'[30]

6. FROM MISSION TO MUSEUM

WITHOUT REFUELLING, A Blackbird had a maximum operational range of some 2,500 miles: maybe two hours' flying time, after which it could simply fall out of the sky like an anvil. Vital as the technicians' and ground crews' efforts were in maintaining their aircraft in peak condition, Habus recognised that their lives depended quite as critically on a tanker keeping its planned mid-air rendezvous with them, day or night. The men who flew the fleet of KC-135Q Stratotankers based at Beale were hand-picked and specially trained airmen like themselves. They followed the Habus around the world on their postings, living and partying together in their exclusive enclaves on base.

In a standard daytime refuelling a Blackbird needed to descend from 80,000 feet to 26,000 feet while losing some 1,500 mph of speed and making a ninety-degree turn on to the refuelling track. It was the job of the RSO in the Blackbird's rear cockpit, relying on the inertial navigation system, to tell the pilot the exact moment to begin his deceleration. It had to be very precisely calculated, and so also had the margin of fuel the aircraft needed to hold in reserve before refuelling. Known as 'Bingo' fuel, this was defined as enough left that in the case of something going wrong with the tanker meet-up the Blackbird would still be able to divert to an emergency base with a minimum of 10,000 pounds of fuel to get safely back to earth. Four and a half tons may sound like a generous margin but a single missed approach and go-around would gobble up one and a half tons of the precious JP-7. Fuel consumption at maximum output was getting on for 8,000 gallons an hour, or roughly twenty-four tons. Blackbirds were thirsty birds, and monitoring fuel consumption was a constant preoccupation of all who flew them. While the aircraft made its descent the RSO would be making radio contact with the tanker, not least to check out the weather conditions far below in order to have some idea of possible turbulence, cross-winds and the general visibility down there.

Once they were at 26,000 feet the RSO would give his pilot the tanker's position a few miles ahead until he could pick it up visually. The pilot then brought the Blackbird up behind and slightly below the tanker, which now had its long refuelling boom extended and lowered. Matching its speed, he would slide up beneath it until they were in 'contact position': the boom's nozzle over the refuelling hatch behind the RSO's cockpit. This manoeuvre required extreme skill because the upward view from the Blackbird's small raked windows was never good and was further restricted by the pilot's space helmet. Most pilots lowered their seat by several inches to get maximum vision. Once the position was held the tanker's boom operator, or 'boomer', watching out of his own window, would plug the nozzle into the Blackbird's receptacle, open the cock and give the pilot the laconic message over the intercom: 'You're taking gas.' The JP-7 was pumped in at a rate of some 6,000 pounds or 2.7 tons a minute. Further skill was required by the Blackbird's crew to compensate for this rapid change in weight and to maintain the aircraft's centre of gravity by ensuring the fuel's even distribution in its tanks, all the while flying a race-track pattern for anything up to twenty minutes while attached to the tanker. After that the pilot would disengage and make sure he was well clear of the tanker before he pushed the throttles forward past full military power to where the afterburners lit with twin thuds and blasted him heavenwards once more with a sigh of relief.

This was taxing enough by day in good conditions. But in 1977 the Air Force's SR-71s at Kadena suddenly found themselves under pressure to carry out night operations in order to demonstrate that they could match the twenty-four-hour reconnaissance ability of satellites. Hitherto, Blackbirds had only flown by day, and from the early years missions were usually planned so they arrived over their targets at midday to take advantage of the best angle of sunlight. Night ops in Blackbirds now presented an extreme challenge; and until night flying was mastered with endless simulator and live practice at Beale, even the most fearless Habu was secretly apprehensive. Operations after dark proved excellent for such things as taking the North Koreans by surprise, but night refuelling undoubtedly presented the aircrews with serious difficulties. Primary among these was disorientation caused by the long descent while turning in pitch darkness. All pilots everywhere know how easy it is to become disoriented, even with the best instrumentation, and Blackbird crews were no exception. The ninety-degree turn was soon dropped, which helped, as did better instrument lighting in the cockpit even though Blackbird aircrew were already plagued by distracting reflections off the windows and the gold-filmed helmet faceplates, a problem that never was completely solved even by day. The tankers also acquired a system of lights on their underside to tell the Habu he was too high, too low or too far off to one side. Even so, night refuelling remained one of those manoeuvres that united tanker and Blackbird crews by more than an extensible boom. Both knew the awful price for miscalculation and their mutual trust was absolute. Amazingly, there was only ever a single recorded loss of a KC-135Q on an operation, and that by day. This occurred in Spain in June 1971 following a successful refuelling mission when the tanker crashed as the result of a mid-air explosion in a fuel tank. The crew of five died.

Things were made still harder when in 1978

men from the National Security Agency dropped
in at Kadena with the information that many of
the 'trawlers' off Okinawa were actually Soviet
spy ships picking up the Blackbirds' radio transmissions. From then on strict radio silence was
observed out of Det. 1, breakable only in the case
of an emergency. This also became the rule at Det.
4 (Mildenhall) in view of the Russian 'trawlers'
known to be monitoring the movements of nuclear
submarines out of Holy Loch. This radio silence
was imposed from taxi-out to recovery, the control
tower using a lamp to signal that it was clear to taxi
or take off. It seems astonishing that Blackbirds
could take off, fly halfway around the planet while
meeting up with tankers to refuel before returning to base and landing, all without a single word
being spoken over the radio. But it was really just
an extension of the godlike independence Habus
anyway felt at 80,000 feet where, in the words of
one of them, 'the world belonged to us'.

Even on the ground it took the best part of
an hour to fuel a Blackbird and needed four
people, including a supervisor. When the amount
in the aircraft's tanks matched that required for
the stated mission a fuel sheet was completed

that itemised everything to the last pound, even including the weight of the pilot and his RSO. After much calculation this would reveal the aircraft's all-up weight and where its centre of gravity ought to be. This was then checked against the cockpit's CG meter reading. If all had gone well the two figures would be identical. But other things beside fuel were needed. Liquid nitrogen for inerting the tanks was added to the two 104-litre reservoirs. These had heater coils that turned the nitrogen into gas that pressurised the entire fuel system. And since Blackbird aircrew breathed pure oxygen, liquid oxygen was pumped into the aircraft's three LOX converters.

The crews' pressure suits, though more comfortable than the type issued to the early U-2 pilots, were still not much fun to spend hours in, and especially not in the Blackbird's cramped cockpits. (It was definitely an advantage to be small and wiry, as it has been for almost all military aviators since 1914.) The longest-ever Blackbird operational flight took place in October 1973 during the Yom Kippur War, when Washington badly needed to know how far Israeli forces had advanced into Egypt. The mission was to have been flown out of Griffiss AFB in New York State with recovery at RAF Mildenhall, but at the last minute the British blocked this. Prime Minister Edward Heath had placed an arms embargo on all the war's combatants and refused permission for the US to use any British base for resupply or intelligence-gathering. The sortie thus had to be flown from Griffiss and back again. Jim Shelton and his RSO, Gary Coleman, duly took off at 01:15 and soon met up with a tanker, which demanded considerable work for both pilots because halfway through refuelling heavy turbulence broke the connection with the tanker's boom. This had to be re-established even as Shelton's stick shaker – a warning device that literally shook his control stick – told him he was on the verge of stalling.

He and Coleman then climbed away, reached Mach 3 and crossed the Atlantic before meeting up with another tanker, this time in Portuguese airspace. After that and once again at cruise altitude and speed Shelton decided on a snack and a drink of water. But nothing so natural was straightforward while wearing a space suit in a Blackbird. He first had to contend with one of NASA's tubes of strained apricots that sprayed everywhere when his drinking tube broke the seal in the cockpit's reduced pressure (equivalent to 26,000 feet). The drinking water went better but in time inevitably led to the problem of peeing. Shelton's own description gives some idea of how very much more there could be to flying a Blackbird than mere piloting:

> The pressure suit has a urine collection device (UCD) built into it. The urine is collected in small plastic bags, nicknamed 'piddle packs', in the lower left pressure suit pocket. When you fill one piddle pack you can put it into the lower right suit pocket. When you fill the second one, you can leave it in the lower left suit pocket. However, if you need to use a third piddle pack, the problem becomes what to do with pack number two in the left pocket. I improvised by hanging the pack on the canopy emergency jettison T-handle, located on the left-side console. It worked fine as long as I didn't have to raise or lower the ejection seat.[31]

But, of course, for all subsequent refuellings he did have to lower the seat and afterwards raise it again.

In this way Shelton progressed, flying the world's most advanced aircraft on a top-secret mission while festooned with bags of urine. The one dangling from the canopy handle needed protecting with one hand as with the other he activated the seat height switch, all the while trying to line the Blackbird up with a tanker.

The third refuelling rendezvous took place off Crete, although it nearly didn't because Spanish Air Traffic Control had delayed permission for the tanker's take-off, and only by pushing it to its never-exceed speed did the captain manage to keep the tryst by a matter of seconds. However, with a full fuel load Shelton now headed down the Suez Canal while in the compartment behind Coleman saw the 'M' light on his ECM panel light up, telling him they were being tracked by radar. To his relief no 'L' light told them that a missile had been launched and he was content to be tracked so long as it stayed that way. Back at Griffiss the intelligence officer had told them that no country had been informed of the flight and a Russian SAM site in Egypt could well take a pot shot at them. Luckily this never happened and the tracking soon stopped.

As he began a 270° right-hand turn to skirt Cairo,

Shelton found himself at a Blackbird equivalent of 'Coffin Corner' that perfectly exemplified the difficulty of flying so close to the aircraft's limits. According to his schedule he needed to maintain his speed at Mach 3.15, so in order to keep this and his altitude in the turn (when an aircraft's wings lose lift) he increased the afterburner to maximum thrust. However, the air temperature outside was warmer than the usual -55°C, requiring additional thrust he no longer had. The choice was to lose either speed or altitude, so he chose the latter. As he lost height to maintain Mach 3.15 a red warning light told him his air speed was now too high for the new altitude. The slightly denser air was causing his engines' compressor inlet temperature (CIT) to go up. As mentioned earlier, Blackbirds were less limited by Mach number than by the temperature of the air as it reached the engines' compressors. The airframe had a design limit of Mach 3.2 although it could be pushed to Mach 3.3, but only if the CIT limit of 427°C was not exceeded. In a dire emergency or in order (in the official parlance) *to exit a hostile area by the most expeditious means,* you could fly for an absolute maximum of one hour with a CIT of up to 450°C provided you *never* exceeded Mach 3.3. An unstart above that speed would almost certainly lead to the aircraft's disintegration and probably that of the crew as well.

So that day above Cairo Shelton completed his lengthy turn with the air speed warning light on all the way until he rolled out level again and used his excess thrust to take them back up to a height where the warning light finally went out. An Egyptian SAM site once again began to track them and, glancing out of his side window, Shelton saw the contrail of what he took to be one of the Egyptian Air Force's Russian fighters a safe 40,000 feet lower. Still scooping up information, the Blackbird overflew Israel and then turned left towards the fourth refuelling near Crete. The intelligence-gathering done, Shelton relaxed enough to have another go at a tube of apricot puree and this time managed to get it to squirt into his mouth through the hole in the faceplate instead of everywhere else. The fifth air refuelling off Portugal also went according to plan, but as they set off back across the Atlantic Shelton filled a fourth piddle pack and was faced with the conundrum of what to do with it. He finally put it in a chart container on top of the instrument panel, praying it wouldn't leak into the circuit breaker panel and blow fuses or start a fire.

The sixth and final refuel was over Canada, and Shelton took on only a small load for the comparatively short run down to Griffiss AFB where Coleman had already ascertained the weather was clear. They duly landed after a flight of eleven hours and nineteen minutes, the longest ever by a Blackbird. If one adds another hour for such things as the pre-flight formalities and taxiing, it has to be imagined what it would be like to remain for all that time strapped into a seat in a small cockpit while wearing a pressure suit, surrounded by piddle packs and smeared with stewed apricot, all the while performing highly skilled tasks including six air-to-air refuellings. Habus deserved every bit of their celebrity.

As a result of their momentous flight Shelton and Coleman were called to the Pentagon to be thanked personally by the chairman of the Joint Chiefs of Staff and shown some of the pictures their Blackbird had taken. These revealed the Israelis had moved much further into Egyptian territory than Golda Meir was admitting and the

State Department promptly used them to pressure her to withdraw. Shelton added: 'I saw one photo I would love to have a copy of for my own collection, but it had *SECRET* stamped all over it. It had both the Pyramids and the Sphinx in the same picture frame, shot from 80,000 feet.'

There was a curious sequel to the mission eleven months later that took place at Farnborough Air Show. Shelton was trying to keep the crowds away from the Blackbird that had just flown from New York to London in a shade under an hour and fifty-five minutes when a man asked him in broken English about SR-71 flights over the Middle East the previous year. Shelton duly said that he had no idea what he was talking about, to which the man replied: 'Don't bullshit me. I'm a MiG-21 squadron commander from Egypt.' Ever security-conscious, Shelton denied knowing anything; but he did wonder whether the man had been flying the aircraft whose contrail he had noticed far below him in October 1973.[32]

★

This mission showed the Blackbird at the zenith

of its powers in the 1970s: reliably able to cross the world at three times the speed of sound and with impunity acquire 'takes' of the utmost political and strategic importance while remaining aloft for an entire day. It was a complete vindication of 'Kelly' Johnson's Archangel 12 design, even if getting to that point had cost a fortune and required techno-logical ingenuity that only the United States could have mustered. There were another fifteen years still to go before the type was officially grounded, in which time Blackbirds went about NATO's and the Pentagon's business while breaking sundry records on the side, many of which seem unlikely now ever to be re-broken. They overflew the Falkland Islands in 1982 and a later mission in April 1986 went to ascertain how much damage the USAF's bombing of Libya had done when eighteen F-111s out of RAF Lakenheath and Upper Heyford launched strikes against Colonel Gaddafi's compound in Tripoli.

But all the time official opposition to this unique aircraft was steadily growing even though in the late 1980s electronic advances had made it possible for the Blackbirds' radar imagery to be relayed digitally in flight for instant interpretation on the ground. This was a blow to the aircraft's opponents who had always claimed the delay in having to process its film rendered the SR-71 outmoded for intelligence gathering. Suddenly it looked as though the Blackbird's usefulness might be extended for years yet. But that was to reckon without its enemies and the Department of Defense's army of bean counters. The 1980s were also a time of major budgetary reviews in the United States, and the military was not exempt. It was regularly emphasised that a single Blackbird had cost the Air Force an astronomical $34 million (roughly $250 million apiece at today's rates). Once again the small SR-71 fleet came under scrutiny by the intelligence community as well as by the Air Force, both eager to cut costs, and it was all too obvious that 'The Program' was on borrowed time. Among chairbound senior ranks of the USAF there was great resentment of the Blackbirds' iconic public status, and particularly of the men who flew them.

By the late 1980s one Habu claimed the Blackbird was now 'a curse word among the Air Force general officer corps' and that its demise was imminent, 'much to the delight of the Air Force bureaucracy'. On 1 October 1989 the USAF suspended all SR-71 activities, except for a few training flights, while it awaited the release of the budget for Fiscal Year 1990. This came within weeks and made clear that all funding for the Blackbird programme was forthwith cancelled. Accordingly, all operations were ordered officially terminated as from 22 November. The following January a dignified and emotional retirement ceremony was held at Beale AFB, the Blackbirds' home. It was attended by representatives from the CIA and Lockheed as well as USAF personnel, and many wept at having to witness what they considered the premature ending of the world's most potent aircraft with years of service still left in it. In truth, an epoch had ended.

'Kelly' Johnson himself had less than a year to live. He was approaching eighty and had expended the energy of several ordinary men on his U-2s and Blackbirds, seeing the projects through seemingly insurmountable technical, financial and political problems. In addition, he had had a hand in the design of aircraft as different as the ubiquitous C-130 Hercules and the first operational true stealth aircraft, the F-117A Nighthawk. Yet undoubtedly his most phenomenal achievement remains to have designed the Blackbird in the early months of 1959, obtained the CIA's go-ahead that July and got this uniquely complex aircraft into the air on 26 April 1962. Those hectic two years and nine months represent a landmark in aviation history. They put to shame the foot-dragging production of virtually every high-performance military aircraft since. They are a testimony to Lockheed's wisdom in giving this brilliant and determined man a free hand to run things according to his own famous '14 Rules of Management', the first of which was 'The Skunk Works manager must be delegated practically complete control of his program in all aspects.' His methods could indeed be autocratic, but his confidence in giving his hand-picked technicians the freedom to solve their own problems rubbed off on them and the results were their own justification. His team had equal confidence in him, not least because he had already designed several outstanding aircraft but because he was an instinctive engineer of genius, with the uncanny natural gift of being able to look at a design on paper and give an instant and accurate assessment of the mass of its various components. He could also tell at a glance whether it would fly.

But by 1990 'Kelly' Johnson's great days were over. Exhausted by his long career, the deaths of his first two wives and the years of his own illness, he died in December that year. The earlier grounding of the SR-71 might have been a cause for grief but by then it would hardly have come as a surprise. Back in November 1987 the first attempts had been made to calculate how much it might cost to shut down The Program. Many Air Force officers at the Pentagon were privately shocked by the idea but as it was enthusiastically promoted by the Chief of Staff himself, General Larry D. Welch, they prudently considered their own careers and 'weathervaned' so as to agree with him. They soon discovered they were expected to perjure themselves by exaggerating The Program's expense. In order to inflate the SR-71's flying-hour costs they added in those of the Blackbird's KC-135Q tanker support as well as of its special maintenance personnel, even though this measure was never applied to other Air Force aircraft such as B-52s or F-15s. It later emerged that the Blackbirds had nearly been axed there and then, and only the personal intervention of CINCLANT (Commander-in-Chief, Atlantic Command) kept them flying for a further year to monitor and track Soviet nuclear submarines.

In a revealing interview in 1991 Ben Rich, 'Kelly'

Johnson's successor at the Skunk Works, recalled:

> In August 1989 General Welch had ordered us to
> give him a cost to destroy all existing SR-71s and
> A-12s in storage both here at Palmdale and at
> Beale. He doesn't want the SR-71s dispersed, but
> destroyed. It took us about ten days to address
> his request. Lockheed's response to General
> Welch for a figure on the destruction of the
> SR-71 fleet was approximately $67 million per
> aircraft. When Welch heard that, he changed his
> mind and said, 'Maybe we should just send them
> all to museums.'[33]

General Welch's preference for a 'scorched earth'
policy was consistent with the order twenty years
earlier to destroy all the Blackbird's jigs, moulds
and dies at the Skunk Works. And such is the nature
of service hierarchies that once the tide of official-
dom had turned against the aircraft in Washington
it became open season for baiting its supporters.
Two former Habus, RSOs who were seconded to
the Pentagon in the late 1980s, retained bitter
memories of the way in which they were singled
out for their reasoned opposition to official Air

Force policy on shutting down the programme. Curt Osterheld and 'Geno' Quist described themselves as dedicated officers in 'loyal opposition' to a policy they felt was seriously mistaken.

> Some officers within the intelligence community saw [the end of the Blackbirds] as the next leap forward for satellite reconnaissance dominance (and their own upward mobility), so they jumped on the 'kill the SR-71 now' bandwagon. Geno and I were convinced that some took a sadistic delight in the SR-71's struggle for survival. I recall a hall meeting with a colonel (who was not a flying officer) in which he sneered at me and Geno and stated, 'It serves you pressure-breathing prima donnas right. I hope you all die.'[34]

On 6 March 1990 a Blackbird on its way to the Smithsonian Museum ended its career in a blaze of glory. On its flight to Dulles Airport, Maryland and flying over the recognised Los Angeles–East Coast course, it established two new world speed records. One was for coast-to-coast (2,086 miles) in one hour, seven minutes and 53.7 seconds: an

average speed of 2,144.83 mph. The other was for
Los Angeles to Washington, DC (1,998 miles) in
one hour, four minutes and 19.89 seconds. It was
the perfect way of cocking a snook at the Pentagon
and its deskbound generals. Far from being obsolete, the Blackbird was a record-breaker right to
the end. In 1995 Congress, fearing the Blackbird's
retirement had been grossly premature, voted
$100 million to reactivate three SR-71s, primarily
for duty over the increasingly unstable Middle East
following Desert Storm, but nothing much came
of it. On 10 October 1997 the Air Force flew a
Blackbird for the very last time. Four days later
President Clinton vetoed the limited reactivation
with immediate effect.

There remained the single aircraft not owned
by the USAF. On 9 October 1999 NASA's lone
SR-71 was flown at Edwards AFB's Open Day. It
was the Blackbird's swansong. Never again would
the spectators feel the very concrete beneath their
feet rumble to the low-frequency thunder of J58s
and watch the twin strings of blue-hot shock diamonds blast that distinctive black shape into the
Californian sky. The ear-battering sound died
and a resounding era in aviation was at an end.

As Habu Richard Graham later wrote: 'This time the Blackbirds will not rise from the ashes. All that remains are memories of the greatest aircraft ever flown. When members of the Blackbird Association meet in Reno for their biennial reunion, stories, tales and legends of the Blackbird abound. They will survive in our hearts and minds for ever... *they* can never be retired.'[35]

7. APOTHEOSIS

I N 1974 THE aftermath of the Watergate break-in led sensationally to President Nixon's resignation to avoid impeachment. It followed revelations that this vengeful man had bugged the Oval Office in the White House, thus nicely illustrating his private paranoia. At the same time the military paranoia that had flourished in the United States for the previous two decades overflowed into American domestic culture generally. The British writer and ex-communist-turned-exposer of Stalin's purges Robert Conquest once observed: 'Every organisation behaves as if it is run by the secret agents of its opponents',[36] which neatly sums up the incestuous nature conspiracy shares with state security. Theories about John F. Kennedy's assassination spawned films in the 1960s and 1970s such as *Executive Action* and *The Parallax View*. Growing public suspicion that a hidden world of rogue intelligence agencies was spying on citizens also made good box office (*The Conversation, Three Days of the Condor*) and came to characterise the febrile tenor of an entire decade. At one point in *Winter Kills* (1979) John Cerruti, a computer fanatic played by Anthony Perkins, claims proudly: 'From our satellite we can watch everything – nasty little wars in Africa, troop movements, ship movements, nuclear tests, the Sinai, the Panama Canal, every little thing. … Even tonight, while most of our workers sleep, *it* goes on.'

In some ways the Blackbird was the perfect expression of *it*, affording a lofty, secretive, all-seeing gaze. But whose gaze? The CIA's? The USAF's? The DIA's? The NRO's, or any other of the sixteen different US intelligence agencies? Come to that, why not SPECTRE's gaze? Or even that of some crazed private-enterprise Jack D. Ripper? Invisible to ordinary mortals, detectable by radar yet untouchable, Blackbirds went about their elevated business by day and night, hoovering up earthbound information that was then interpreted by mysterious agencies with their own political and strategic agendas. Maybe from 80,000 feet they permitted the overview that puts everything into perspective and reveals the Truth.

One melancholy truth revealed by the story of the SR-71 was that there is nothing so hi-tech that it can't be superseded. The Age of Paranoia gave way eventually to our present Age of Stupidity, when we have blithely enabled acned adolescents in frowsty bedrooms to impartially read our e-mails, raid our bank accounts and steal secret files from the Pentagon. The target of physical objects seen from the air has been considerably supplanted by that of encrypted computer files. It is likely that as early as the mid-1960s, even as it had barely begun, the Blackbird's career was already doomed by a mixture of macropolitics, departmental squabbling and matters of cost, but above all by burgeoning satellite technology. So it goes. All aircraft, particularly military ones, are designed for a stated requirement with clear specifications as to performance, weight, load capacity, serviceability and cost. If at some future date that requirement changes or no longer exists, or the aircraft can no longer perform it as well or as cheaply as more modern alternatives, it becomes redundant and is withdrawn from service. A few examples wind up in museums or become gate guardians of airfields that were once associated with them. In Europe, and especially in Britain, most are either sold off to lesser air forces or chopped up for scrap.

In the United States obsolete and redundant warplanes frequently wind up parked in the famous boneyard attached to Davis-Monthan AFB outside Tucson, where the dry desert air preserves them free of rust and most decay. They may be cannibalised for spare parts to keep others of their kind in service: the USAF's ageing but still viable fleet of B-52 bombers is to some extent kept air-worthy with parts taken from the endless glittering ranks of aircraft parked wing to wing in neat rows under the Arizonan sun.

None of this is true of the Blackbird fleet, with the exception of the seventeen TAGBOARD D-21 reconnaissance drones stored at Davis-Monthan. Of the thirty surviving aircraft, all but one are on display in the United States. The sole exception is in the Imperial War Museum's American hangar at Duxford, England, in recognition of the type's long service at Detachment 4, RAF Mildenhall, twenty-five miles away. The scrap value of the remaining Blackbirds' tons of titanium must be considerable, but they are, of course, untouchable. Aside from that, no Blackbird has parts that will ever be needed by any other type. Like dinosaurs, these magnificent beasts can never be brought back to life. It is not that their genetic code is lost or too badly damaged for accurate retrieval (although some of it undoubtedly is), nor that it might not be theoretically possible at astronomical expense to clone the sundry special lubricants and sealants, the tyres and windows, plastic composites and paints. It is that Blackbirds no longer have a role that cannot be achieved by other, far cheaper and more efficient means. Claims to the contrary by devotees are merely sentimental. True, a resurrected SR-71 would have immense crowd-pleasing cachet at air displays even though there seems little point in restricting an aircraft designed for Mach 3.2 at 80,000 feet to tame flypasts at subsonic speed. It would be like watching Formula 1 cars limited to thirty miles an hour and in both cases would soon ruin the engines. (And it is pointless even to *think* about the cost of fuel and maintenance, let alone of training pilots and keeping them current on type to meet safety standards, especially since no SR-71 simulator has survived.) The Blackbird is dead. And yet it lives on.

★

Sixty-odd years have passed since 'Kelly' Johnson first drew the twelfth Archangel design while sitting in his Skunk Works office and recognised it as the definitive version. The original wind-tunnel model now looks like a sculptor's maquette: as much a work of art as of science. And like a maquette it was subject to a minor tweak or two before being scaled up and cast in titanium. The artist himself has been dead for over a quarter of a century. Now, in common with any great work of art, his Blackbird seems genuinely timeless. In this respect it is utterly unlike one of those Detroit Baroque cars of the same period. Such space-age chrome-and-fins Americana is instantly datable to a glamorous suburban dream long since banished by the grimly earthbound realities of economics and environmentalism, not to mention changing taste. But to walk around a Blackbird is to be still mesmerised by its aesthetics, its aura of agelessly wicked power. One may know its engines have been removed, its hydraulic plumbing is corroded, the sealant in its tanks brittle and shrunken; but the monstrous energy of its lines is undiminished. It hasn't aged a day and probably never will.

What is more, its capability will never be exceeded. No air-breathing, turbojet-engined aircraft will ever fly faster. Half a century ago the Blackbird set its trisonic engine's physical limits at a shade over Mach 3.3 and there is no longer any reason to try to go beyond that. No doubt a new generation of drones and commercial transports will eventually arrive that fly much faster and far higher; but they will be powered by other means, whether by rocket or ramjet or scramjet or something Green and science fictional like ion beams. Very likely they will skitter around the planet on the thin edge of space before re-entering the thicker atmosphere, the leading edges of their flying surfaces glowing cherry-red. Children will probably grow up taking it for granted that on a good day a London to Sydney trip will take forty-five minutes' flight time, a shade over an hour if there's a solar headwind.

Yet it is worth betting that the ageing Blackbirds in their museum hangars or standing on cracked tyres in the Californian sun will still retain something of their former magic. This is partly because their mysterious black looks derived directly from a requirement for stealthy spying in an age of paranoia. The very design has *secrecy* written all over it: conceived in secret and flown in secret in order to gather secrets. The sheer effort and achievement of turning that requirement into record-breaking fact at the extreme limit of a dozen different technologies somehow shows, and will likely remain intact across the years. Of all the world's aircraft types ever built a mere double handful – the majority American – might qualify for the epithet 'great', whether on account of their performance, ruggedness, longevity in service or even just looks. Somehow the Blackbird transcends all of them and remains in a class of its own, still surrounded by a mythic glow. Even the crews who flew it in that far-off, pre-computerised-cockpit age seem to stand apart in a special niche. Like knights in their pressurised armour, or simply in their orange flying suits, the Habus retain a certain mystique if only because theirs was a comparatively small brotherhood. In just over thirty years only 141 men ever passed the exacting selection and training to pilot the fifty Blackbirds built in the type's three main variants; and their ranks are steadily thinning.

Strange that political and military panic should have spurred a single nation to produce two prodigious technological masterpieces in the same decade: Apollo 11 and the Blackbird. Maybe after all there is something to be said for paranoia.

ACKNOWLEDGEMENTS

Warm thanks to Lindsay Peacock for some declassified OXCART documents, the colour photograph of the RB-47H at Upper Heyford, and for generous and expert advice on aviation and wine-tasting.

BIBLIOGRAPHY/SOURCES CONSULTED

Byrnes, Donn A. and Hurley, Kenneth D., *Blackbird Rising* (Sage Mesa, 1999)

Crickmore, Paul F., *SR-71 Blackbird* (Osprey, 2016)

Goodall, James and Miller, Jay, *Lockheed's SR-71 'Blackbird' Family* (Aerofax/Ian Allan, 2002)

Graham, Richard H., *SR-71 Blackbird. Stories, Tales and Legends* (Zenith, 2002)

Graham, Richard H., *The Complete Book of the SR-71 Blackbird* (Zenith, 2015)

Helms, Richard with Hood, William, *A Look Over My Shoulder: A Life in the Central Intelligence Agency* (Random House, 2003)

I. F. Stone's Weekly, 28 July 1969

Jenkins, Dennis R., *Lockheed Secret Projects* (MBI, 2001)

Jensen, J. R., *Remote Sensing of the Environment: An Earth Resource Perspective* (Prentice Hall, 2000)

Johnson, C. L. and Smith, Maggie, *Kelly* (Smithsonian Books, 1989)

Johnson, R. W., *Look Back in Laughter: Oxford's Postwar Golden Age* (Threshold, 2015)

Pace, Steve, *Lockheed Skunk Works* (MBI, 1992)

Page, Sir Frederick, *Daily Telegraph* obituary of 7 May 2005

Pardew, Connie: 'A-12 40th Anniversary' (<area51special-projects.com/pardew.html>)

Pedlow, Gregory W. and Welzenbach, Donald E., *The Central Intelligence Agency and Overhead Reconnaissance: The U-2 and OXCART Programs, 1954–1974* (History Staff, CIA, Washington, DC, 1992)

Rich, Ben R. and Janos, Leo, *Skunk Works: A Personal Memoir of My Years at Lockheed* (Little, Brown, 1994)

Stanley, Roy M., *Asia from Above* (AuthorHouse, 2006)

Whittell, Giles, 'The spy who fell to earth', *The Times*, 15 January 2011

GLOSSARY

AAA	Anti-aircraft artillery
AAM	Air-to-air missile: a rocket fired by one aircraft at another
ADP	Advanced development projects: Lockheed's 'Skunk Works' division
AFB	Air Force Base
CG	Centre of gravity
CIA	Central Intelligence Agency
CIT	Compressor inlet temperature: the temperature of the air as it reaches a turbojet engine's compressor
DIA	Defense Intelligence Agency
DMZ	Demilitarised Zone: in the Vietnam War, the dividing line between North and South Vietnam
DoD	Department of Defense (US)
ELINT	Electronic intelligence (gleaned principally from the analysis of signals)
HUMINT	Human intelligence (as gathered by

flesh-and-blood spies in seedy cafés)

IAS   Indicated air speed. This is the speed displayed to the pilot. Because it is obtained by measuring the external air pressure in a forward-facing tube (the pitot head) it only equals the aircraft's actual speed through the air (TAS or true air speed, q.v.) at sea level. As altitude increases the density of the air reduces and this in turn reduces the pressure in the pitot even if the aircraft's speed through the air is unchanged. When above sea level IAS will therefore always be less than TAS. At 40,000 feet the TAS is twice the IAS displayed to the pilot

IC   (United States) Intelligence Community. A federation of sixteen US Government intelligence agencies

ICBM   Intercontinental ballistic missile

IMINT   Imagery intelligence (information obtained from satellite and aerial photographs)

INS   Inertial navigation system

Kt   Knot, or nautical miles per hour. The air speed gauges of most subsonic aircraft are calibrated in knots rather than mph. The nautical mile being slightly longer than its terrestrial cousin, a speed of 450 kt is equivalent to 518 mph

Mach Note that a Mach number is *not* a measurement of speed but the ratio of an aircraft's speed to that of sound in the air through which it is flying. This varies according to local temperature. See footnote on p. 28

NATO North Atlantic Treaty Organisation

NORAD North American Aerospace Defense Command

NRO National Reconnaissance Office. One of the 'Big Five' US Government intelligence agencies. Builds, operates and monitors spy satellites

RCS Radar cross-section: a measurement of how visible something is to radar

SAC Strategic Air Command (1946–92). Was responsible for the delivery of all US land-based nuclear weapons, whether via ICBM or aircraft. Also responsible for reconnaissance aircraft and aerial tankers. Motto: 'Peace is Our Profession'

SAM Surface-to-air missile. The Soviet SAM that downed Gary Powers' U-2 was an SA-2

SAS Stability augmentation system. Essentially a computerised system that could react more quickly than a Blackbird's pilot to correct most instability

TAS   True air speed. An aircraft's actual speed through the air. Note that because the mass of air may itself be moving TAS will not necessarily equate to the aircraft's ground speed

TDY   Temporary duty

TEB   Triethylborane. A chemical that bursts into flame on exposure to air. Used to ignite a Blackbird's JP-7 fuel and afterburners

TEOC   Technical objective camera. It had a forty-eight-inch focal length lens and used nine-inch-wide film

USAF   United States Air Force

NOTES

1. See Fred Kaplan, 'Truth stranger than "Strangelove"', *International Herald Tribune*, 13 October 2004.
2. Defense Budget Hearings before the House Subcommittee on Defense Appropriations, released 14 April 1964.
3. Pedlow, Gregory W. and Welzenbach, Donald E., *The Central Intelligence Agency and Overhead Reconnaissance: The U-2 and OXCART Programs, 1954–1974* (Washington, DC: History Staff, Central Intelligence Agency, 1992), pp. 61–2.
4. Whittell, Giles, 'The spy who fell to earth', *The Times*, 15 January 2011.
5. Ibid., pp. 124–5.
6. Quoted in Goodall, James and Miller, Jay, *Lockheed's SR-71 'Blackbird' Family* (Aerofax/Ian Allan, 2002), p. 13.
7. Quoted in Graham, Richard H., *SR-71 Blackbird. Stories, Tales and Legends* (Zenith, 2002), p. 167.
8. Goodall and Miller, op. cit., p. 15.
9. Johnson, C. L. and Smith, Maggie, *Kelly* (Smithsonian Books, 1989), pp. 136–7.
10. Ibid., p. 140.
11. Ibid., p. 142.

12. Goodall and Miller, op. cit., p. 22.
13. Ibid.
14. Ibid.
15. Connie Pardew, 'A-12 40th Anniversary' (<area51specialprojects.com/pardew.html>)
16. See Kenneth S. Collins in Graham, Richard H., *SR-71 Blackbird* (Zenith, 2002), p. 22.
17. Ibid., pp. 22–3.
18. Ibid., p. 24.
19. This often-cited claim was made, inter alia, by Bill Park, the A-12's second test pilot.
20. Rich, Ben R. and Janos, Leo, *Skunk Works: A Personal Memoir of My Years at Lockheed* (Little, Brown, 1994), p. 220.
21. Helms, Richard, with Hood, William, *A Look Over My Shoulder: A Life in the Central Intelligence Agency* (Random House, 2003), p. 266.
22. Slightly edited from Byrnes, Donn A. and Hurley, Kenneth D., *Blackbird Rising* (Sage Mesa, 1999), pp. 271–2.
23. Ibid., pp. 208, 209.
24. *Daily Telegraph* obituary of Sir Frederick Page, 7 May 2005.
25. Pedlow, Gregory W. and Welzenbach, Donald E., *The CIA & Overhead Reconnaissance: The U-2 & OXCART Programs 1954–74* (CIA, 1998), p. 308.
26. Quoted in Jensen, J. R., *Remote Sensing of the Environment: An Earth Resource Perspective* (Prentice Hall, 2000).
27. *I. F. Stone's Weekly*, 28 July 1969.
28. Pedlow & Welzenbach, op. cit., p. 313.
29. Goodall and Miller, op. cit., p. 65.

30. Graham, R. H., *SR-71 Blackbird: Stories, Tales and Legends* (Zenith, 2002), p. 218.
31. Ibid., p. 91.
32. Ibid., p. 94.
33. Goodall and Miller, op. cit., p. 68.
34. Graham, op cit., p. 202.
35. Ibid., p. 245.
36. Quoted in Johnson, R. W., *Look Back in Laughter: Oxford's Postwar Golden Age* (Threshold, 2015).

IMAGE CREDITS

Black and white images

p.12 Photo by Everett Historical.

p.17 Photo by Granger Historical Picture Archive / Alamy Stock Photo.

p.27 Photo by US Air Force.

p.29 Photo by US Air Force.

p.32 Photo by National Museum of the US Air Force.

p.36 Photo by US Navy.

p.42 Photo by NASA.

p.52 Photo by Sovfoto / UIG via Getty Images.

p.58 Photo by US Air Force.

p.70 Image by CIA.

p.73 Photo by Granger Historical Picture Archive / Alamy Stock Photo.

p.74 Photo by PF-(aircraft) / Alamy Stock Photo.

p.76 Photo by Sovfoto / UIG via Getty Images.

p.81 Photo by CIA.

p.86 Photo by NASA.

p.101 Photo by Keystone / Stringer.

p.104 Photo by CIA / Roadrunners Internationale,1962.

p.107 Photo by US Department of Defense.

p.148 LOU Collection / Alamy Stock Photo.

Colour images

Plate section 1

1. Photo by US Air Force.
2. Photo by Shutterstock.
3. Photo by USAF.
4. Photo by US Air Force.
5. Photo by Jack Friell via Lindsay Peacock.

Plate section 2

1. Photo provided by Wikimedia Commons.
2. Photo provided by Wikimedia Commons.
3. Photo provided by Wikimedia Commons / taken by Triddle.
4. Photo by LOU Collection / Alamy Stock Photo
5. Photo by NASA.
6. Photo provided by Wikimedia Commons / taken by Andy Webby.
7. Photo by Museum of Flight / CORBIS / Corbis via Getty Images.

Plate section 3

1. Photo by RichardBakerUSA / Alamy Stock Photo.
2. Photo by CORBIS / Corbis via Getty Images.
3. Photo by PJF Military Collection / Alamy Stock Photo.
4. Photo by USAF / Judson Brohmer.
5. Photo by Greg Mathieson / Mai / Mai / The LIFE Images Collection / Getty Images.
6. Photo by NASA.

INDEX

Illustrations are denoted by the use of *italics*.

Aircraft are entered under their model number.